Making Wood Trucks & Construction Vehicles

Reg Martin

 Sterling Publishing Co., Inc.   New York

Library of Congress Cataloging-in-Publication Data

Martin, Reg.
 Making wood trucks & construction vehicles.

 Includes index.
 1. Wooden toy making. 2. Trucks. 3. Construction
equipment. I. Title. II. Title: Making wood trucks
and construction vehicles.
TT174.5.W6M368 1987   745.592   87-10260
ISBN 0-8069-6570-3 (pbk.)

Contents

Color section follows page 32.

Introduction

The projects in this book range from the easy flatbed trailer to the more complex crane. But most of the projects have one thing in common—wheels. You can probably buy appropriate wheels at hobby shops, but I prefer to make my own using a 2 ⅛" hole saw for the 2" wheels. All the other wheels and discs I drew out with a compass, rough-cut with a saw, and then sanded to final contour on the table saw by inserting a sanding wheel. You can leave the wheels as is or add "tread" to your design.

You should carefully fit all moving parts and check them for ease of movement prior to final assembly. It's not always easy to hit all the specified di-

mensions dead on, but what's most important is building the toy so that it works and the satisfaction you get out of building it yourself. The beauty of wooden toys is that if a part breaks, you can easily repair it.

I used red oak for all the toys in this book, and finished them with a spray Varathane. As the toys age, the color deepens and they become very rich in appearance.

I hope you get as much joy and satisfaction out of doing these projects as I did. However, the look in your child's eyes as you give him or her a completed toy will be reward enough for your efforts.

Projects

SEMI-CAB—STYLE 1

Illus. 1. Semi-cab—style 1

1. Start with part 10. Make it out of three pieces laminated together. Shape each piece before gluing. Drill all holes. You will have to rout out the hitch area and fill it back in to desired specified dimensions (see Section A-A in Illus. 3) before drilling the rear axle hole.

2. Install remaining parts in this order: 2 and 3, 4, 8, 5, 6, 9, 1, and 7. The exact location of parts 4, 5, and 6 is up to you.

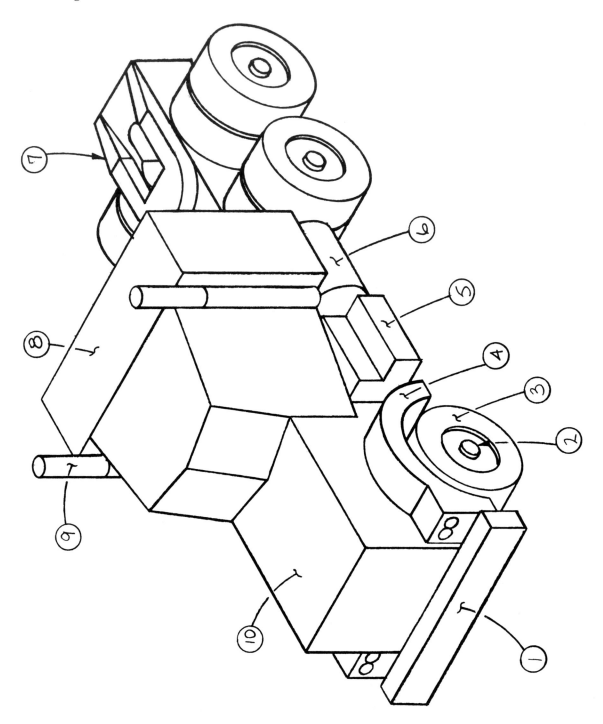

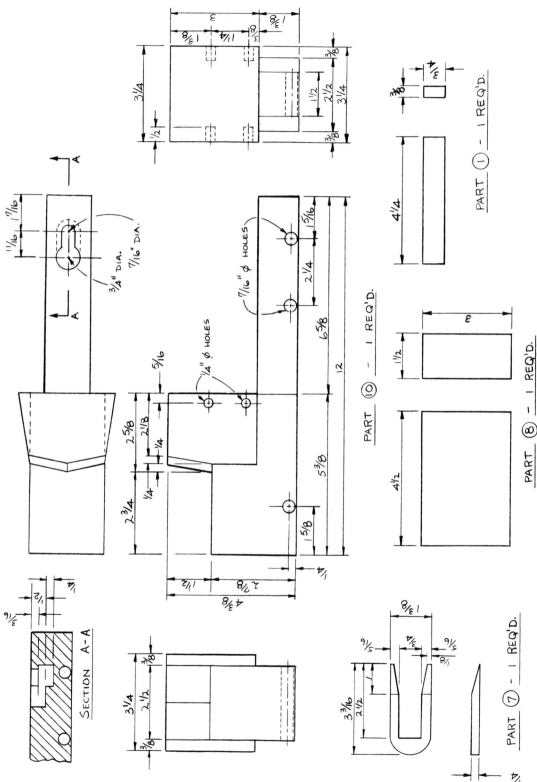

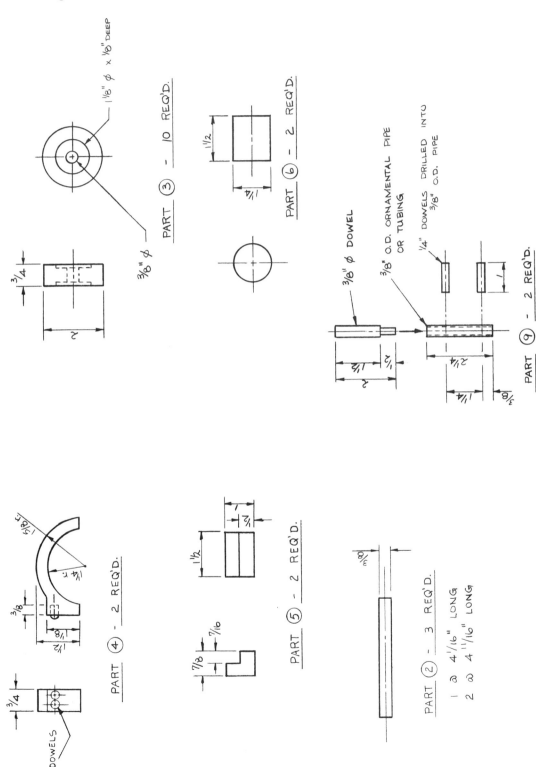

SEMI-CAB—STYLE 2

Illus. 5. Semi-cab—style 2

1. Start with part 6. Make cutouts for wheel assembly and part 7 (see dimensions in Illus. 7). Upper ¾" piece of part 7 should be preshaped before being laminated. Drill all holes. You can add ⅛" × ⅛" strips to simulate ladders.

2. Fit part 7 to part 6 after routing and drilling all holes. You have to rout out the hitch pin hole and then fill it back in to specified dimensions before drilling the rear axle hole (see Section A-A in Illus. 8).

3. Install remaining parts in this order: 3 and 4, 5, 9, 8, 2, and 1.

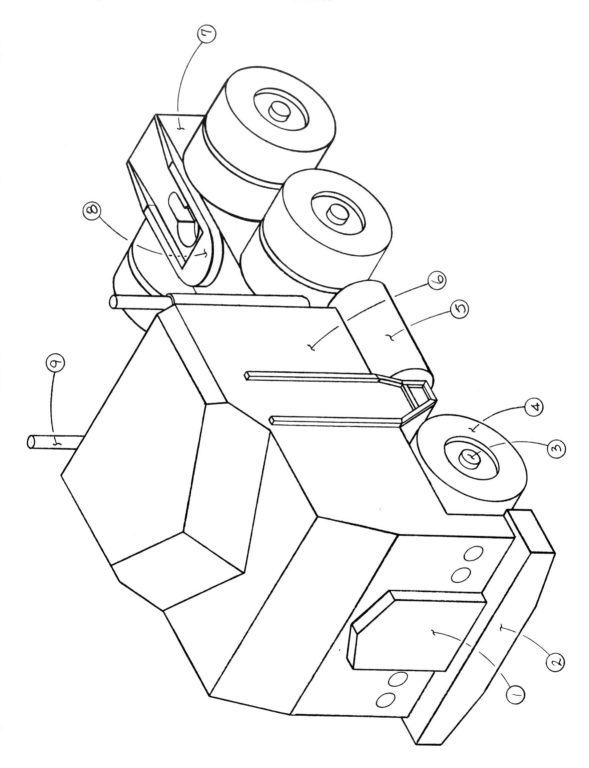

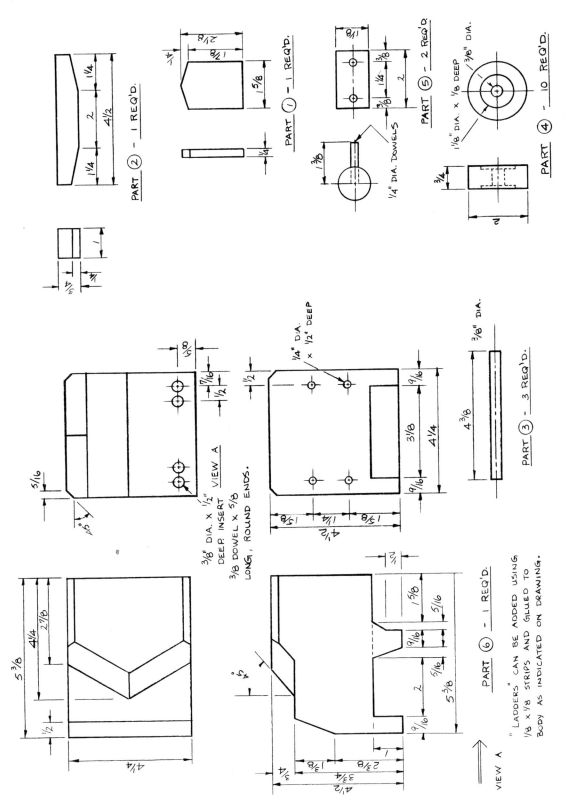

PART ② - 1 REQ'D.

PART ① - 1 REQ'D.

PART ⑤ - 2 REQ'D.

¼" DIA. DOWELS

1⅛" DIA. x ⅛ DEEP

⅜" DIA.

PART ④ - 10 REQ'D.

PART ③ - 3 REQ'D.

⅜" DIA. x ½" DEEP INSERT ⅜ DOWEL x ⅝ LONG, ROUND ENDS.

VIEW A

¼" DIA. x ½" DEEP

PART ⑥ - 1 REQ'D.

VIEW A

"LADDERS" CAN BE ADDED USING ⅛ x ⅛ STRIPS AND GLUED TO BODY AS INDICATED ON DRAWING.

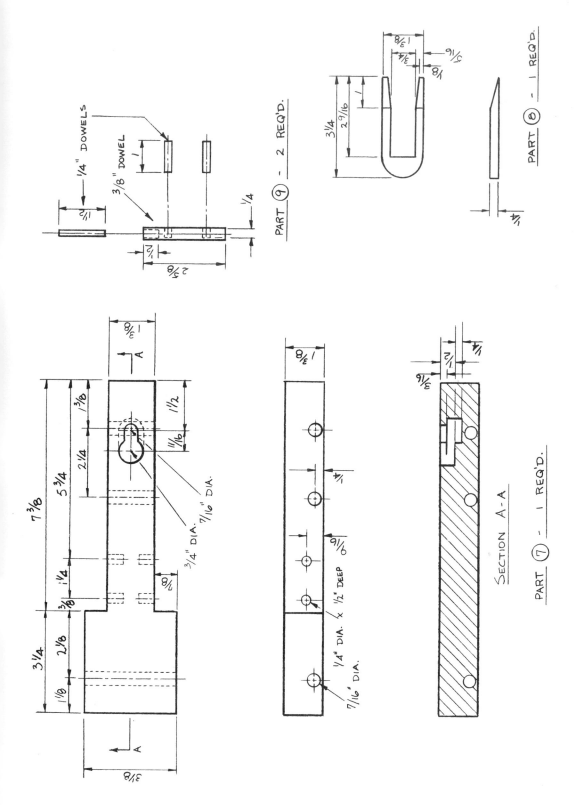

PART ⑨ - 2 REQ'D.

PART ⑧ - 1 REQ'D.

PART ⑦ - 1 REQ'D.

SECTION A-A

BOX TRAILER

Illus. 9. Box trailer

1. Start with part 3. Cut in dado and drill roller holes. After installing parts 3a and 3b, install conveyor belt. Take some 2"-wide ribbed elastic, stretch it around the rollers, and then sew it together. Make sure the seam is neat and smooth or it may hang up on the rollers.

2. Install parts 4 and 5 about ⅛ of an inch from the end of part 3.

3. Install parts 9, 1, 13, and 2. Make sure the door slides smoothly before gluing the parts together.

4. Install remaining parts in this order: 7 and 8, 10, 12, 6, and 11. You will install part 10 far enough back so that it won't interfere with the end of the semi-cab. Where you place part 12 is up to you.

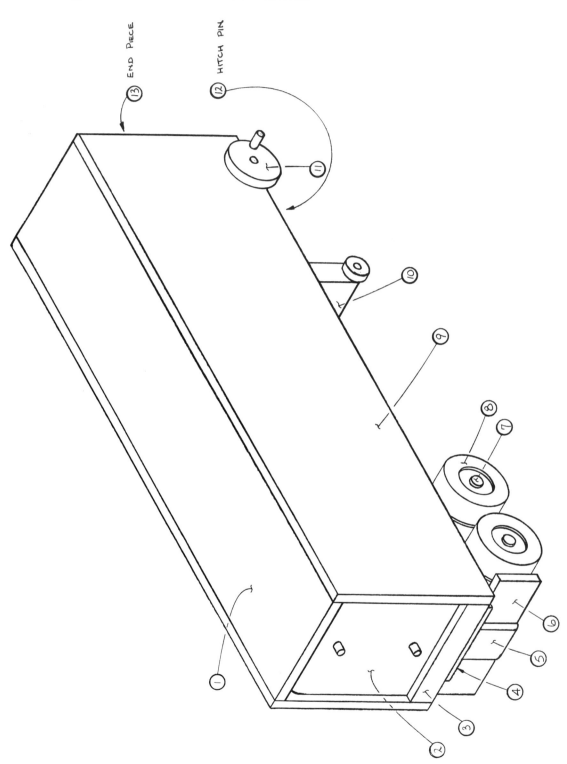

Illus. 10

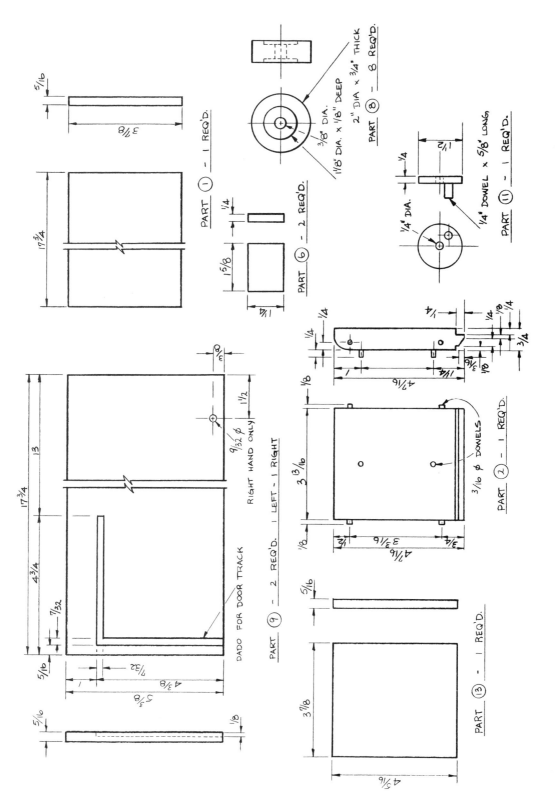

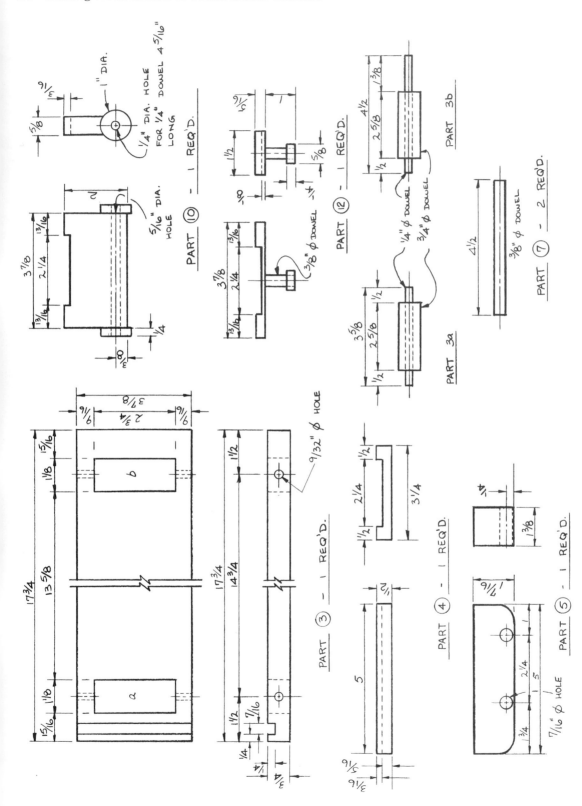

Illus. 12

FORKLIFT

Illus. 13. Forklift

1. Start with part 13. Cut and sand to shape as required. Then glue on upper two pieces as indicated in Illus. 15.

2. Drill axle holes in part 11 and fit to part 13. Glue into place.

3. Fasten part 5 to part 11 with screws or dowels.

4. Install parts 6, 7, and 12.

5. Construct fork assembly (parts 2, 3, and 4). Slide onto part 5. Be sure to wax sliding parts for ease of operation.

6. Install pulley (part 1).

7. Install remaining parts (8, 9, 10, and 14), paying attention to the notes in Illus. 16.

8. Tie on fairly heavy string to spool and to eye on part 4.

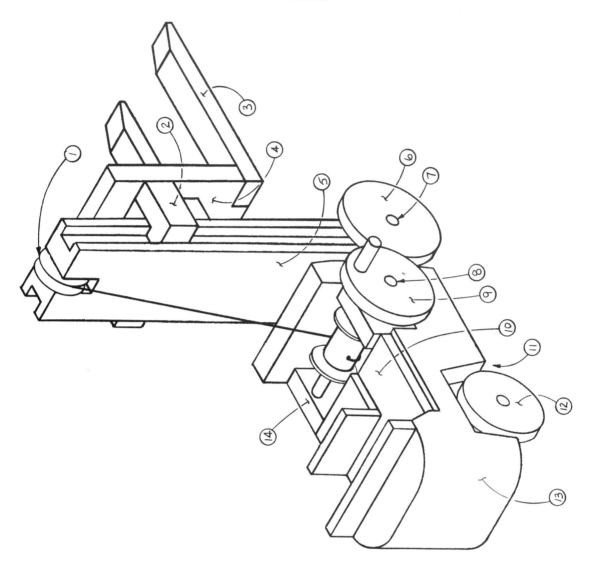

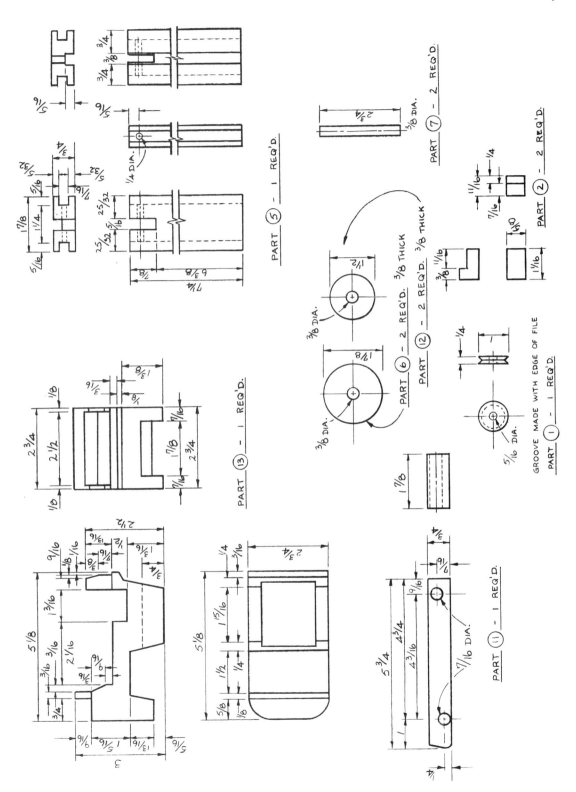

NOTES

(a)(b)(c) INSTALL PART 14. THEN SLIDE (GLUE) PART 9 ONTO PART 8. PASS ASSEMBLY THROUGH PART 14 RIGHT SIDE, THROUGH SEWING SPOOL, THROUGH SPRING, INTO PART 14 LEFT SIDE.

- SPOOL SHOULD HAVE 1/16" DIA. HOLES DRILLED AT ONE END 3/8" FROM CENTER AS IN (d).

- FASTEN SPOOL TO SHAFT.

- SPRING MUST BE FAIRLY WEAK.

- INSERT 1/16" DIA. NAIL INTO HOLE DRILLED IN PART 14 PROTRUDING 1/8". DO THIS PRIOR TO GLUING PART 9 ONTO 8.

- FASTEN PART 4 TO 3 USING SCREWS.

- FASTEN PART 4 TO PART 2 USING SCREWS. INSTALL 2,3,4 ONTO PART 5 BEFORE INSTALLING PART 1.

- INSTALL PART 5 ON TOP OF 11 WITH SCREWS, BEING CAREFUL NOT TO DRILL INTO FRONT AXLE.

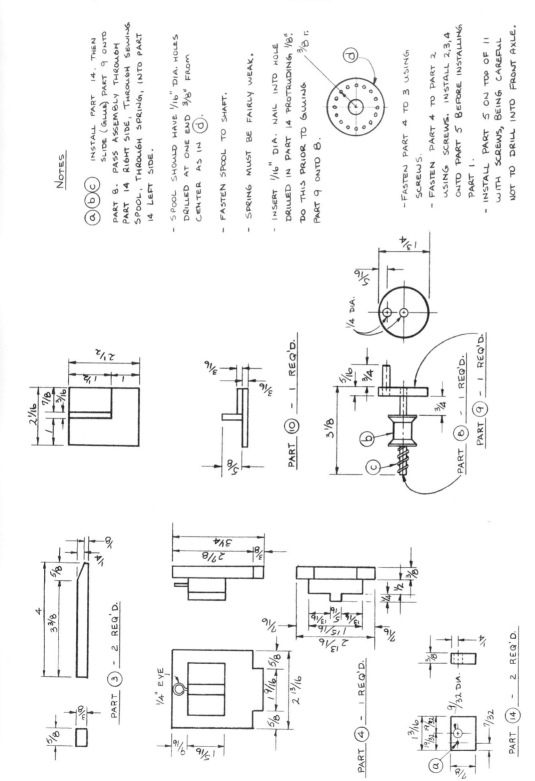

Illus. 16

TANK TRAILER

Illus. 17. Tank trailer

1. Start with part 7. Turn to specified shape and dimensions on a lathe. Laminate upper portion onto main cylinder after running rabbets as indicated (see details in Illus. 19). Bore all holes.

2. Proceed with part 9 and check for fit.

3. Fasten part 4 to part 7 with screws or dowels.

4. Install parts 1, 2, and 3.

5. Install part 6. Location is at your discretion. Test location by fitting trailer to semi-cab.

6. Install part 5. Location to suit your own taste. Position far enough back so as to not interfere with semi-cab.

7. Fit part 8 to part 7. Check for smooth sliding action. After installation, you may want to insert small dowel or finish nail in rabbet to prevent lid from sliding off.

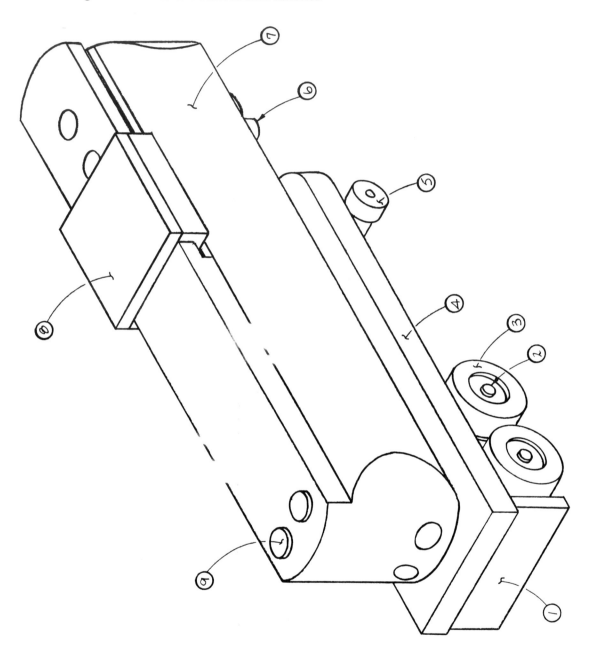

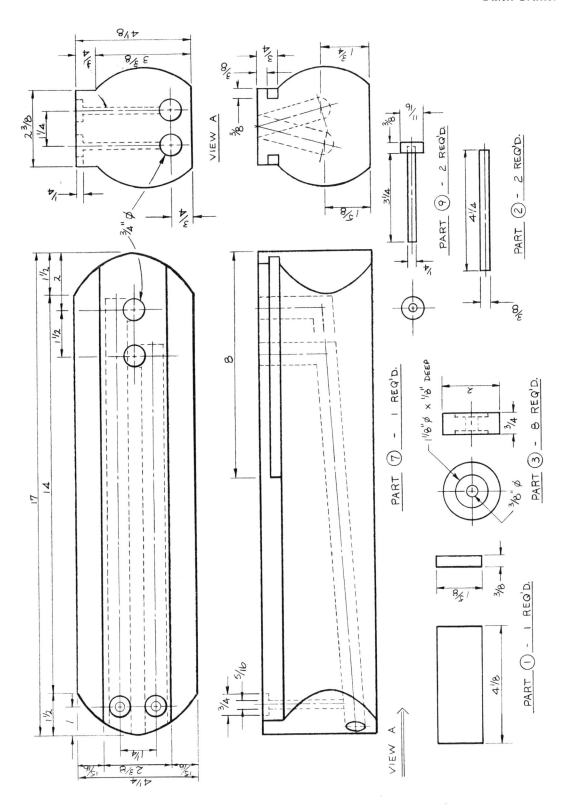

VIEW A

PART 9 - 2 REQ'D.

PART 2 - 2 REQ'D.

PART 7 - 1 REQ'D.

1⅛" φ × ⅛" DEEP

⅜" φ

PART 3 - 8 REQ'D.

PART 1 - 1 REQ'D.

VIEW A

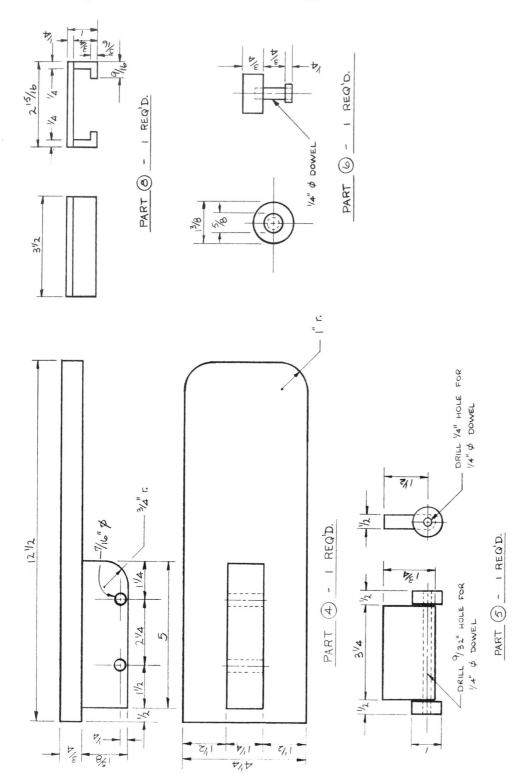

PART ⑧ – 1 REQ'D.

PART ⑥ – 1 REQ'D.

¼" ⌀ DOWEL

PART ④ – 1 REQ'D.

PART ⑤ – 1 REQ'D.

DRILL ¼" HOLE FOR ¼" ⌀ DOWEL

DRILL 9/32" HOLE FOR ¼" ⌀ DOWEL

Illus. 20

TOW TRUCK

Illus. 21. Tow truck

1. Start with part 12. Shape to specified dimensions. Cut dado and drill all holes.

2. Fasten part 13 to part 12 with screws and/or dowels.

3. Assemble part 9.

4. Install part 6 to part 12.

5. Fasten part 9 to part 13 with screws and/or glue.

6. Install parts 7, 10, and 11.

7. Install remaining parts in this order: 3 and 4, 2, 1, 5, and 8.

8. Tie heavy string to the spool. Design of the hook is up to you. *Note:* Part 10 is made from ⅜″-diameter dowel.

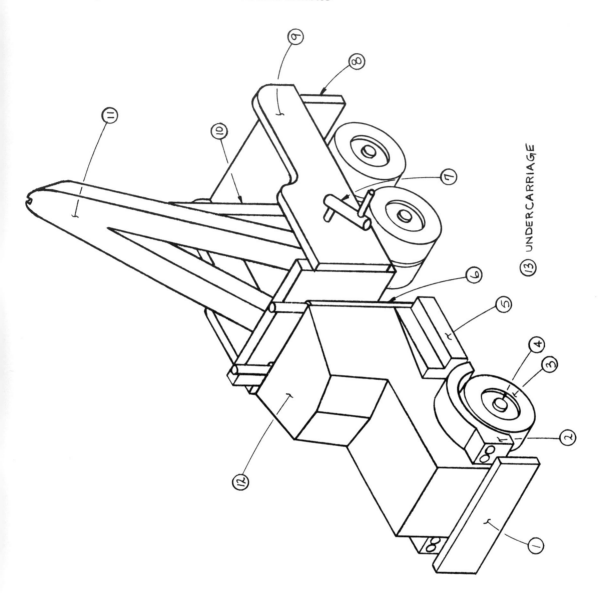

13 UNDERCARRIAGE

Illus. 22

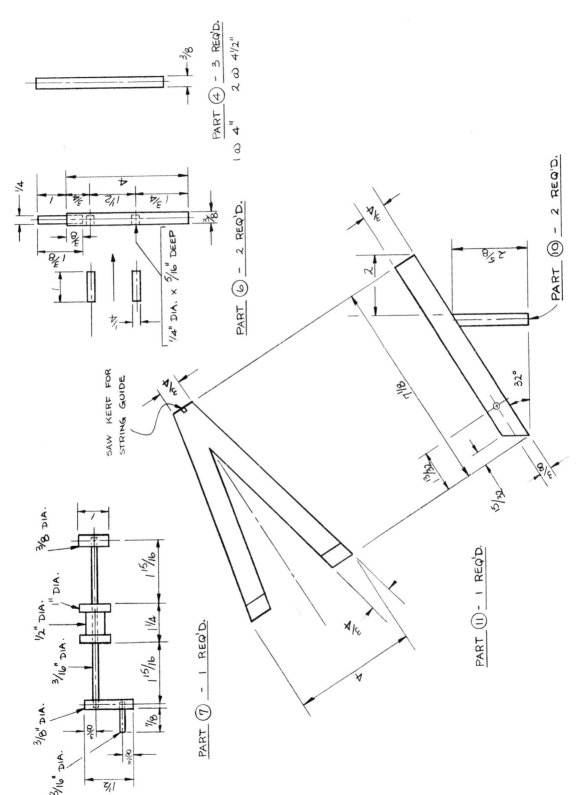

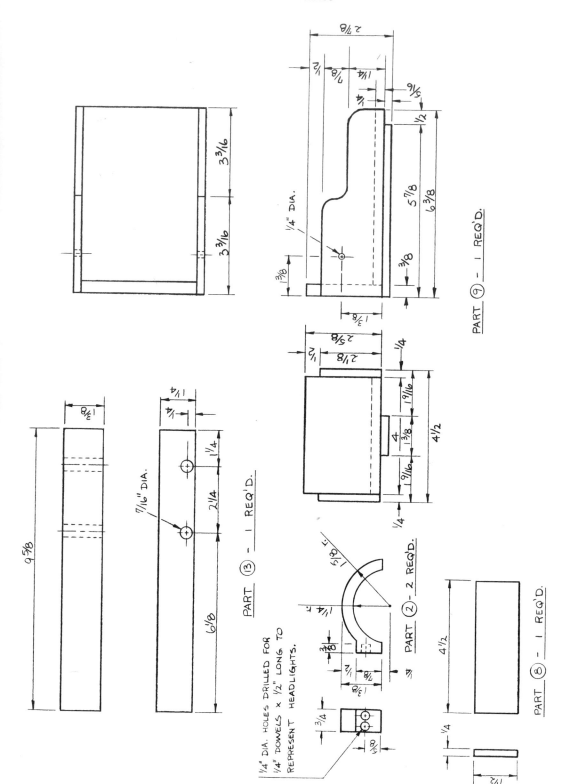

PART ⑨ — 1 REQ'D.

PART ⑬ — 1 REQ'D.

PART ② — 2 REQ'D.

PART ⑧ — 1 REQ'D.

¼" DIA. HOLES DRILLED FOR ¼" DOWELS x ½" LONG TO REPRESENT HEADLIGHTS.

Illus. 24

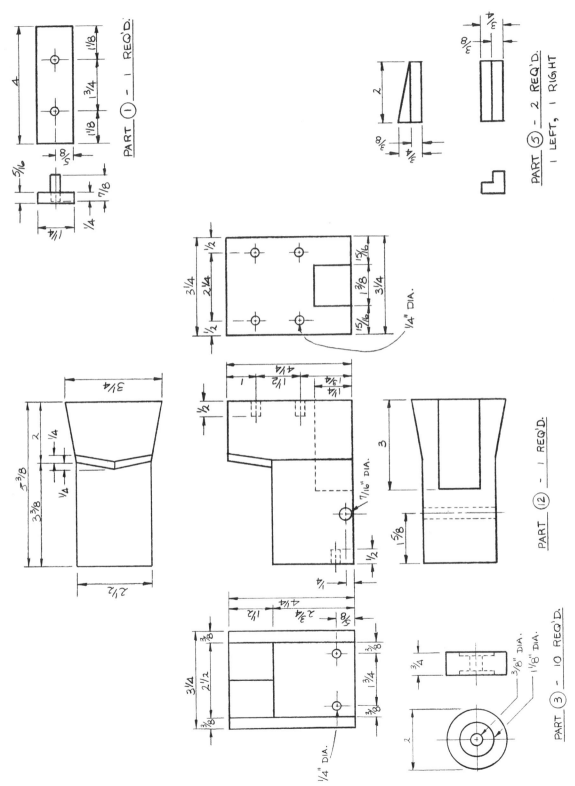

PART ① - 1 REQ'D.

PART ⑤ - 2 REQ'D.
1 LEFT, 1 RIGHT

PART ⑫ - 1 REQ'D.

PART ③ - 10 REQ'D.

Illus. 25

FLATBED TRAILER

Illus. 26. Flatbed trailer

1. Start with part 4. Run the two rabbets and then laminate the chassis to the bottom as indicated on drawing. Drill holes in chassis before laminating.

2. Install part 1 onto part 2.

3. Fasten part 2 to part 3 and then part 3 to part 4 with plugged screws or dowels.

4. Install parts 5, 6, and 7.

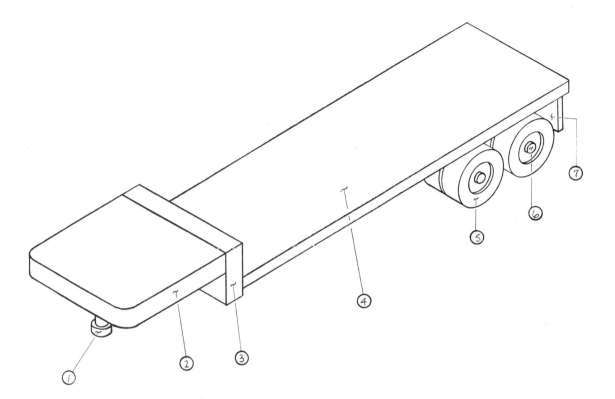

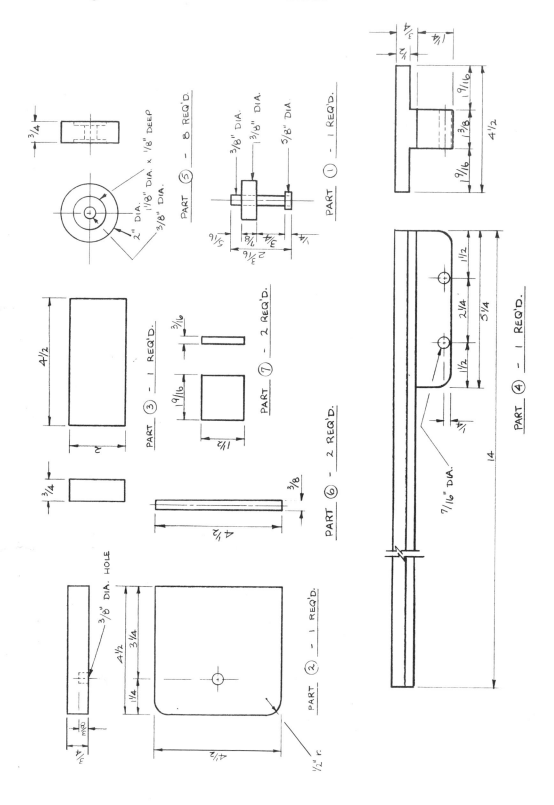

PART (5) - 8 REQ'D.

PART (1) - 1 REQ'D.

PART (3) - 1 REQ'D.

PART (7) - 2 REQ'D.

PART (6) - 2 REQ'D.

PART (4) - 1 REQ'D.

PART (2) - 1 REQ'D.

Illus. 28

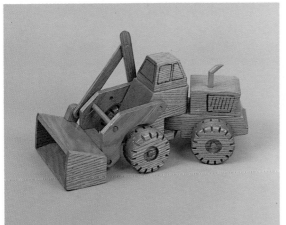

Illus. 1. Loader

Illus. 2. Tow truck

Illus. 3. Dump truck

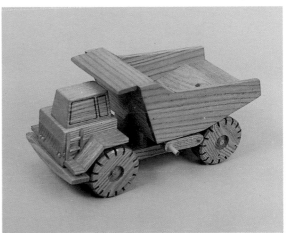

Illus. 4. Mining truck

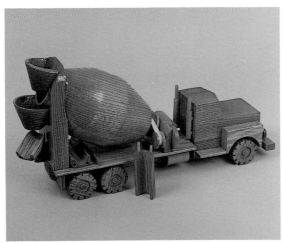

Illus. 5. Cement mixer

Illus. 6. Tractor

Illus. 7. Road packer and grader

Illus. 8. Semi-cab—style 2, low-bed trailer, and bulldozer

Illus. 9. Semi-cab—style 1 and tank trailer

Illus. 10. Sand trailer, sand truck, and semi-cab—style 1

Illus. 11. Box trailer and semi-cab—style 1

Illus. 12. Lumber truck and forklift

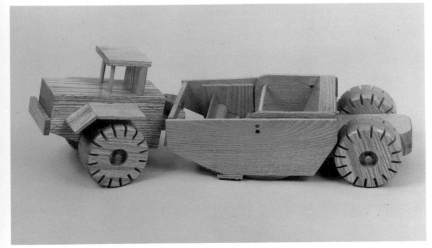

Illus. 13. Earth mover

Illus. 14. Semi-cab—style 1 and flatbed trailer (carrying a hi-hoe)

Illus. 15. Log loader and logging-truck cab and trailer

SAND TRUCK

Illus. 29. Sand truck

1. Start with part 5. Shape as specified. Drill all holes.

2. Install parts 7 and 8.

3. Install parts 3 and 4. Make sure part 3 can slide in and out far enough to release and lock gate (part 4). Sliding dowel (part 3) under part 5 locks gate shut. Sliding dowel out from under part 5 releases gate to open.

4. Install parts 2, 9, and 10.

5. Install parts 6 and 1.

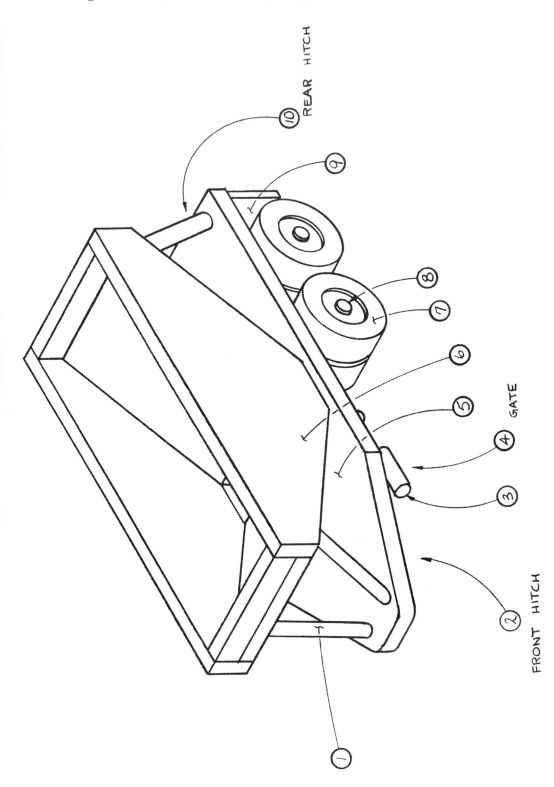

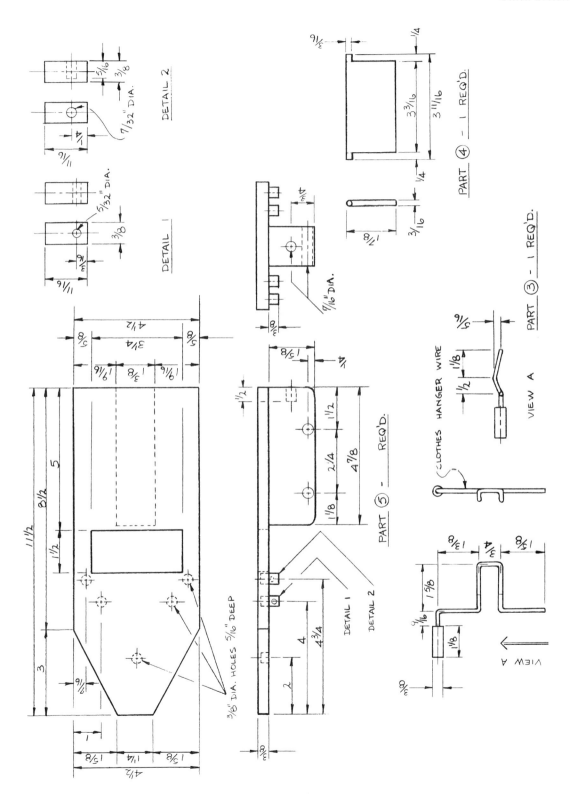

Illus. 31

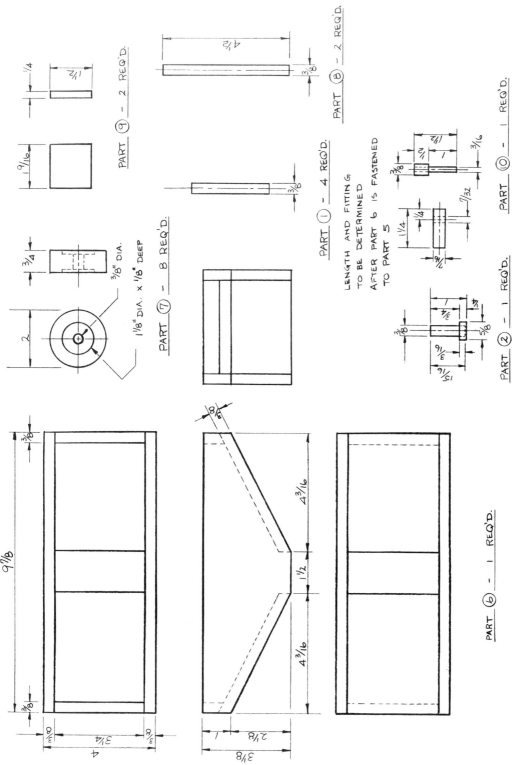

Illus. 32

SAND TRAILER

Illus. 33. Sand trailer

1. Start with part 7. Drill all holes.

2. Install parts 2, 3, and 4. Make sure front axle assembly can pivot freely.

3. Install parts 5 and 6. Part 5 should have enough room to slide in and out.

Sliding in locks the gate shut; sliding out releases gate to open.

4. Install part 9.

5. Assemble part 8.

6. Install parts 8 and 1.

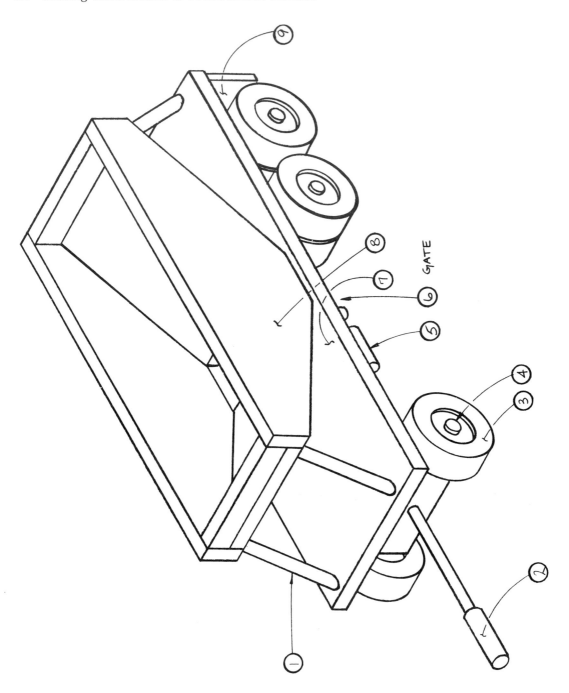

GATE

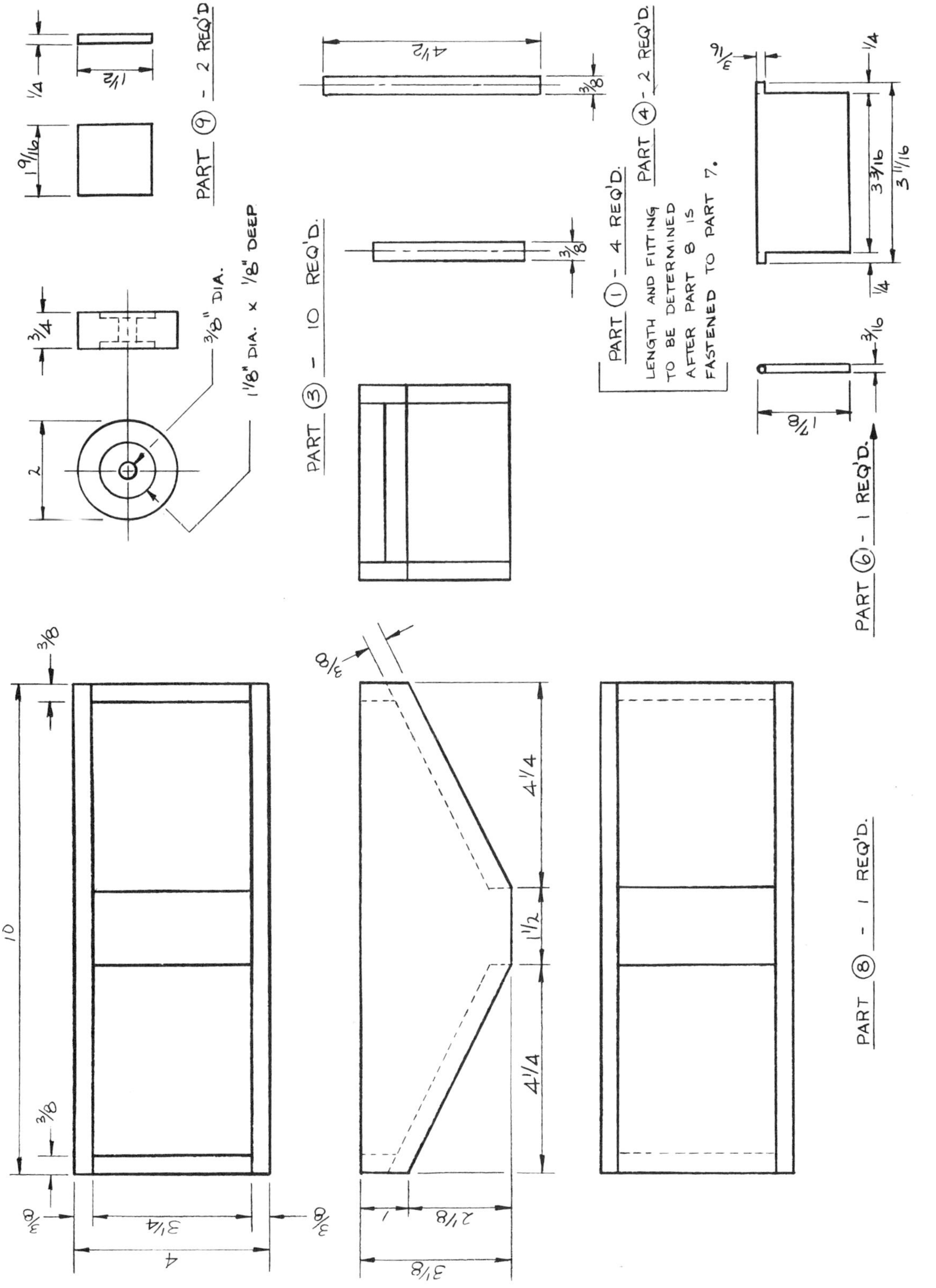
PART (9) - 2 REQ'D
3/8" DIA.
1 1/8" DIA. x 1/8" DEEP
PART (3) - 10 REQ'D.
PART (1) - 4 REQ'D.
LENGTH AND FITTING TO BE DETERMINED AFTER PART 8 IS FASTENED TO PART 7.
PART (4) - 2 REQ'D
PART (6) - 1 REQ'D.
PART (8) - 1 REQ'D.

Illus. 35

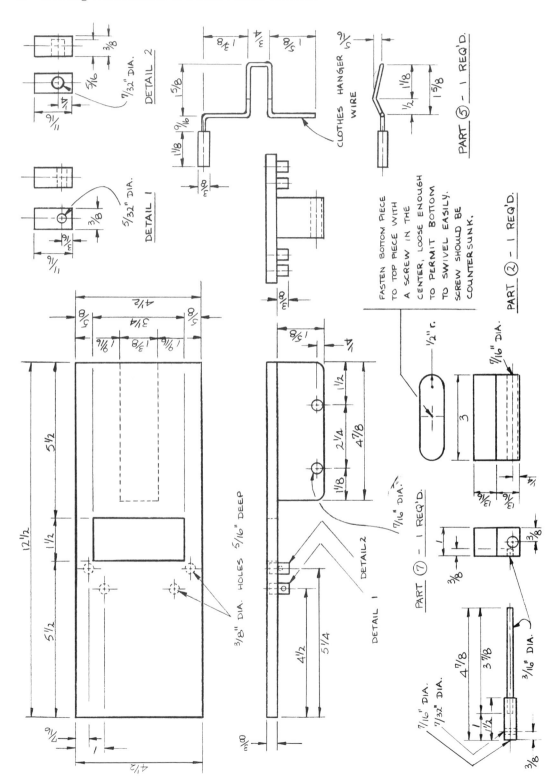

Illus. 36

LOADER

Illus. 37. Loader

1. Start with part 6. Cut and shape to specified dimensions. Drill all holes.

2. Glue part 7 onto part 6.

3. Cut and shape part 3 to specified dimensions. Drill all holes.

4. Connect part 3 to part 6 with dowel, as noted in Illus. 39.

5. Glue part 8 onto part 3.

6. Install parts 4 and 5.

7. Assemble bucket (part 1) and connect remaining parts together (parts 2, 9, 10, and 11), paying attention to notes in Illus. 40.

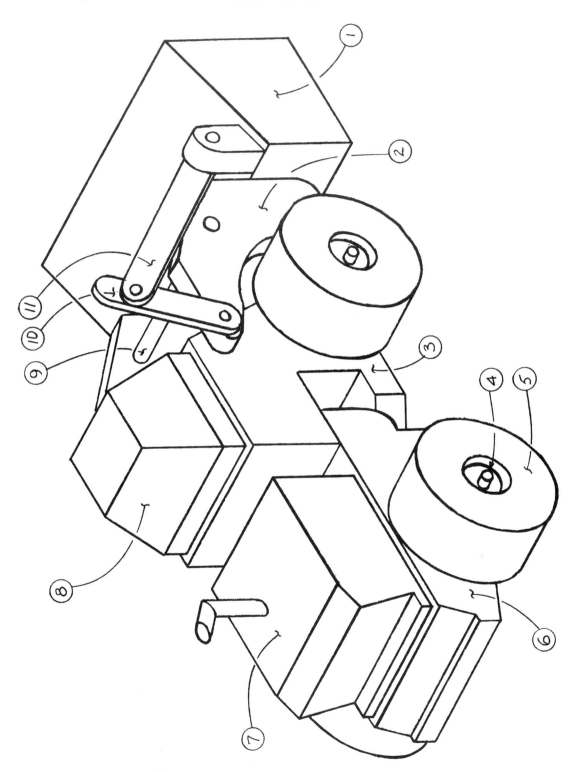

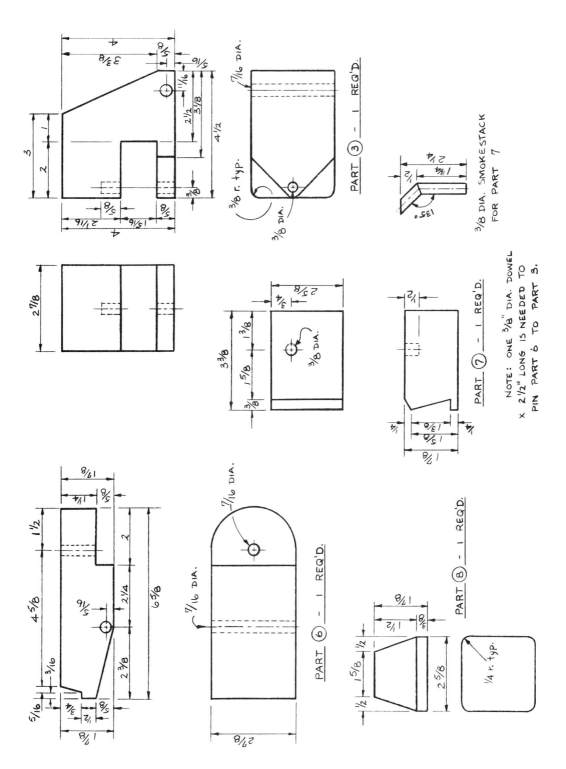

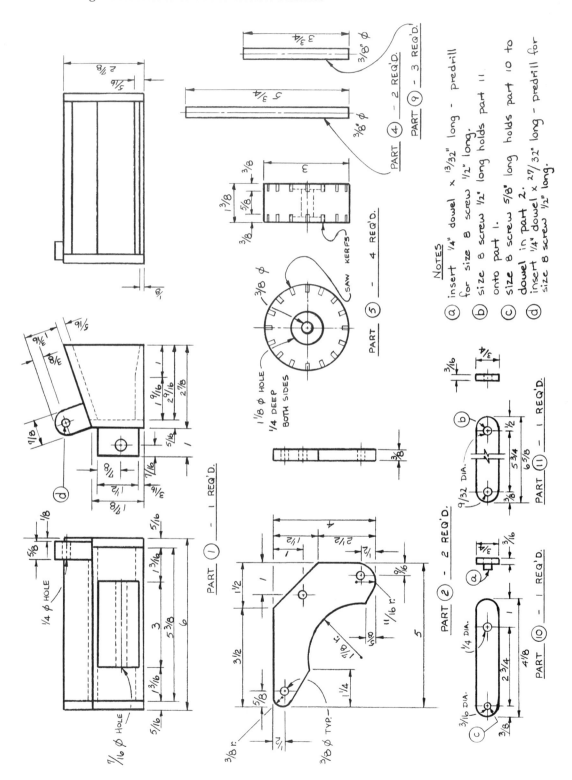

NOTES

ⓐ insert ¼" dowel x ¹³/₃₂" long - predrill for size 8 screw ½" long.

ⓑ size 8 screw ½" long holds part 11 onto part 1.

ⓒ size 8 screw ⅝" long holds part 10 to dowel in part 2.

ⓓ insert ¼" dowel x ²⁷/₃₂" long - predrill for size 8 screw ½" long.

PART ④ - 2 REQ'D.

PART ⑨ - 3 REQ'D.

PART ⑤ - 4 REQ'D.

PART ① - 1 REQ'D.

PART ② - 2 REQ'D.

PART ⑩ - 1 REQ'D.

PART ⑪ - 1 REQ'D.

Illus. 40

DUMP TRUCK

Illus. 41. Dump truck

1. Start with part 13. Cut and shape to specified dimensions. Cut in dado and drill all holes. Upper cab part is laminated.

2. Cut dado into part 7 and drill all holes. Fit and glue part 7 into part 13.

3. Install part 14.

4. Glue part 1 onto part 3 and then fasten whole assembly onto part 14.

5. Install gate (part 2).

6. Assemble remaining parts in this order: 5 and 6, 8, 11, 10, 9, 4, and 12.

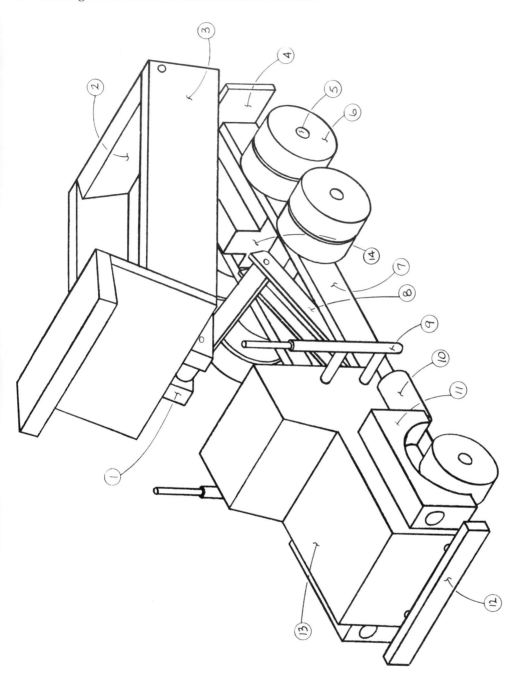

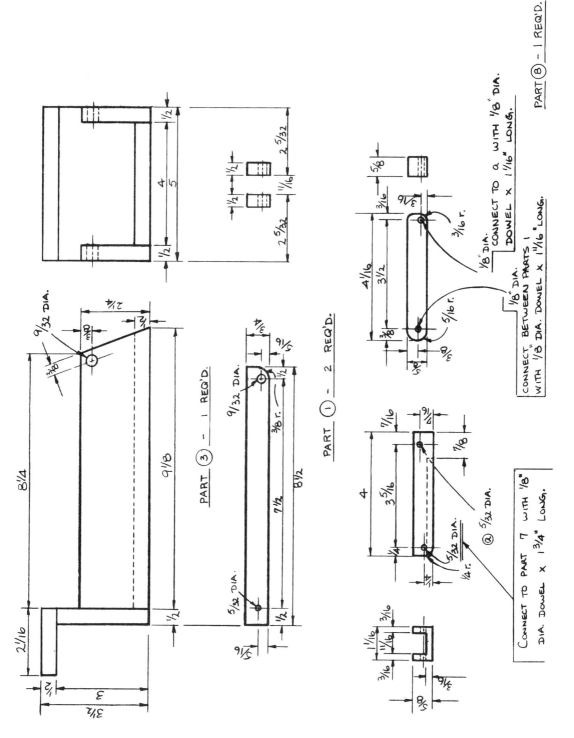

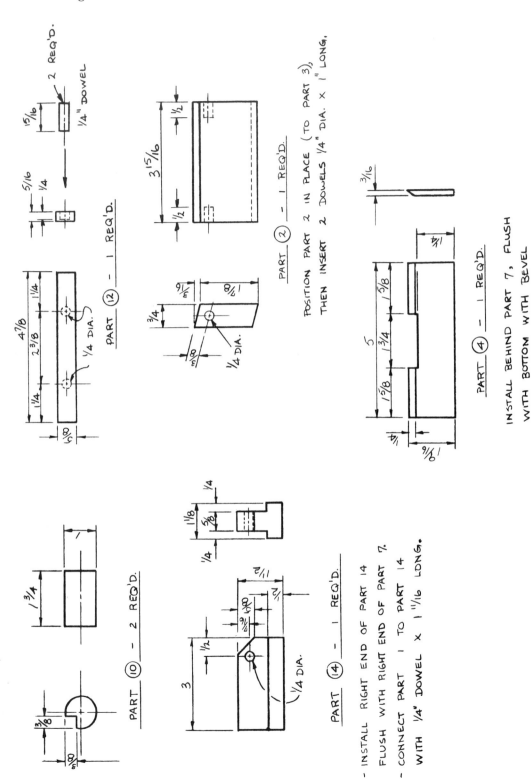

PART ① - 2 REQ'D.

2 REQ'D.
¼" DOWEL
⁵⁄₁₆

PART ⑫ - 1 REQ'D.
5/16   ¼
4⅞   1¼   2³⁄₈   ¼
⅝
¼ DIA.

PART ② - 1 REQ'D.
3¹⁵⁄₁₆   ½   ½
POSITION PART 2 IN PLACE (TO PART 3),
THEN INSERT 2 DOWELS ¼" DIA. × 1" LONG.

PART ④ - 1 REQ'D.
3/16   ¼
5   1⅝   1¾   1⅝
¼   1⁹⁄₁₆
INSTALL BEHIND PART 7, FLUSH
WITH BOTTOM WITH BEVEL
FACING OUTSIDE.

PART ⑩ - 2 REQ'D.
1   ¾   ⅜   ⅝
¼ DIA.
⅜   1⁹⁄₁₆   1⅞
½

PART ⑭ - 1 REQ'D.
¼   1⅛   ⅝   ¼
1½   ½   ⅜   ⁵⁄₁₆   ½
3   ¼ DIA.
- INSTALL RIGHT END OF PART 14
  FLUSH WITH RIGHT END OF PART 7.
- CONNECT PART 1 TO PART 14
  WITH ¼" DOWEL × 1¹¹⁄₁₆ LONG.

Illus. 44

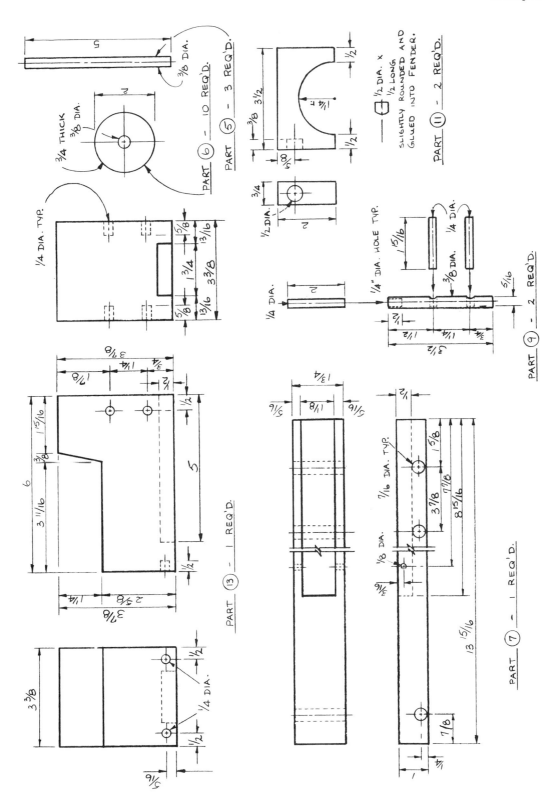

MINING TRUCK

Illus. 46. Mining truck

1. Start with part 1. Cut to specified dimensions. Drill all holes. You can add ladder to passenger side as well as driver side, or use none at all; it's up to you.

2. Assemble part 7.

3. Install parts 5, 6, and 7.

4. Install parts 3, 4, 2, and 8.

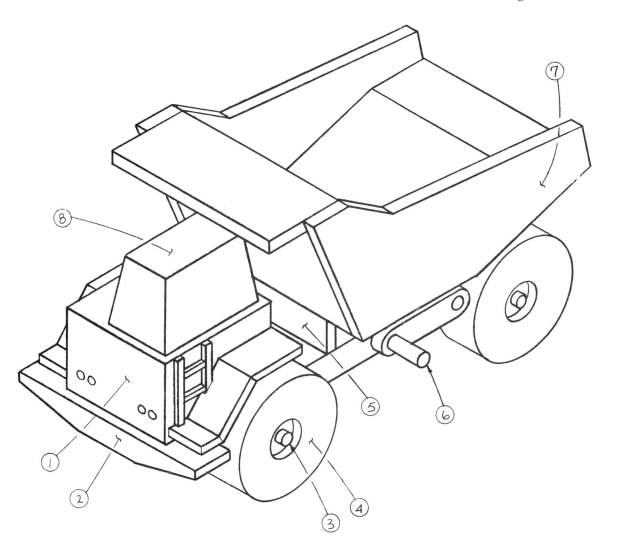

Illus. 47

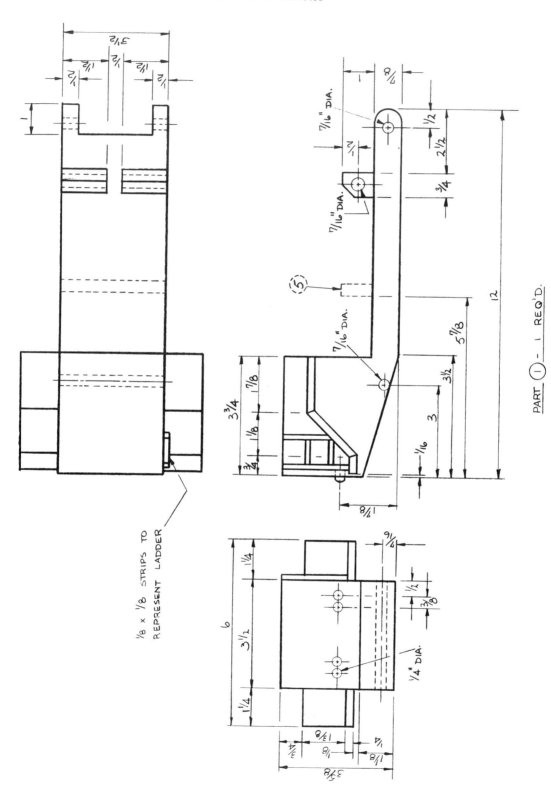

PART 1 - 1 REQ'D.

Illus. 48

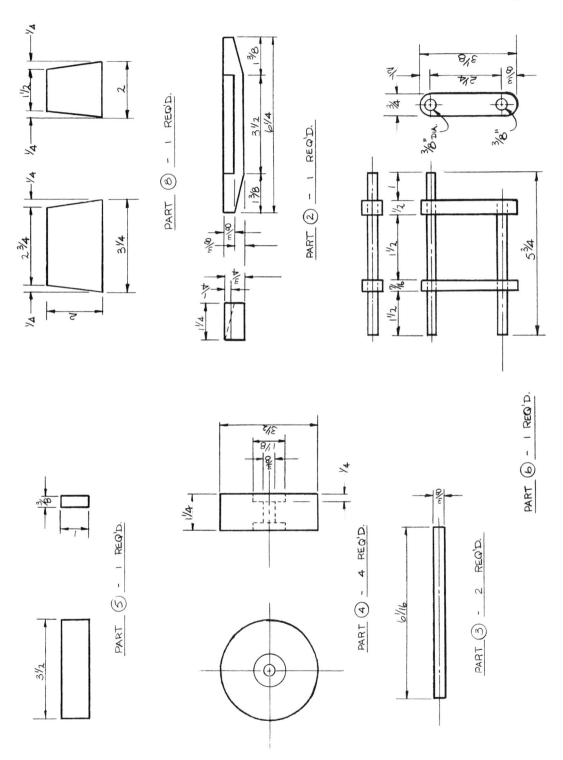

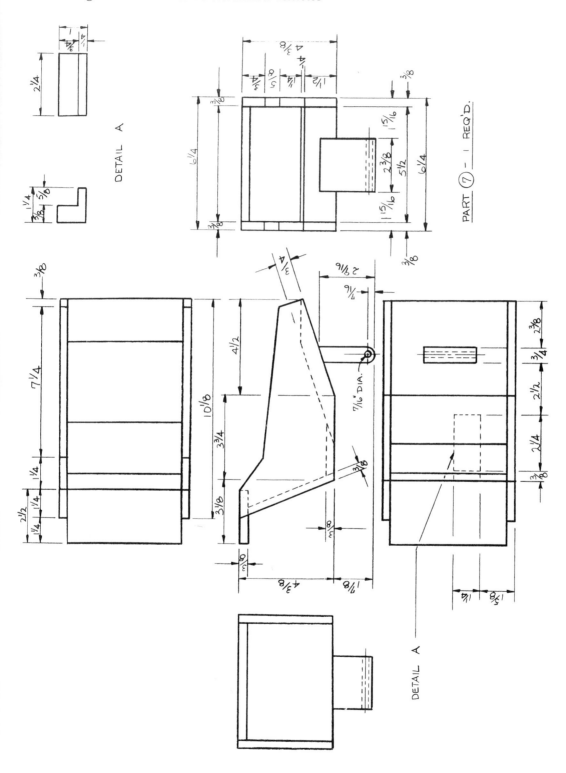

DETAIL A

PART ⑦ — 1 REQ'D.

DETAIL A

Illus. 50

EARTH MOVER

Illus. 51. Earth mover

1. Start with part 2. Cut and shape to specified dimensions. Drill all holes.

2. Install parts 1 and 3.

3. Assemble part 7 along with part 4. They have to be assembled together.

4. Install part 6 to part 7. Location to suit your own taste.

5. Assemble part 5 and install onto part 7, with dowel sliding through both part 7 and part 5 acting as pivot.

6. Install parts 8 and 9.

7. Connect part 7 to part 2 with ⅛"-diameter dowel that is ⅞" long, as indicated in Illus. 53.

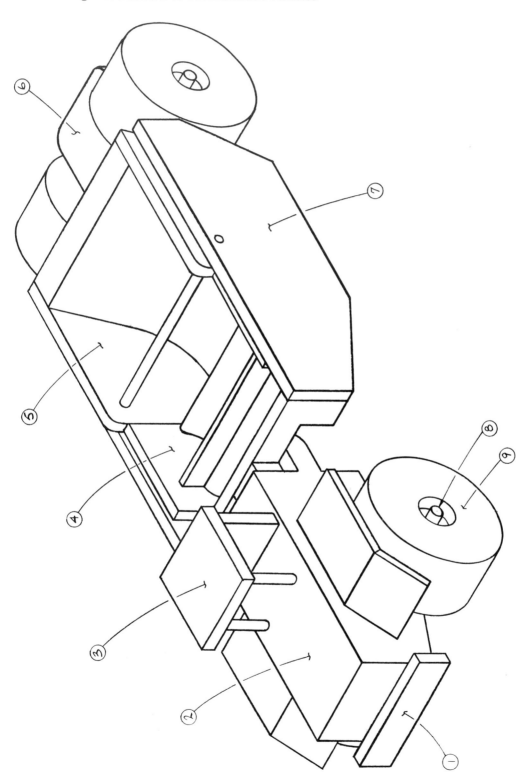

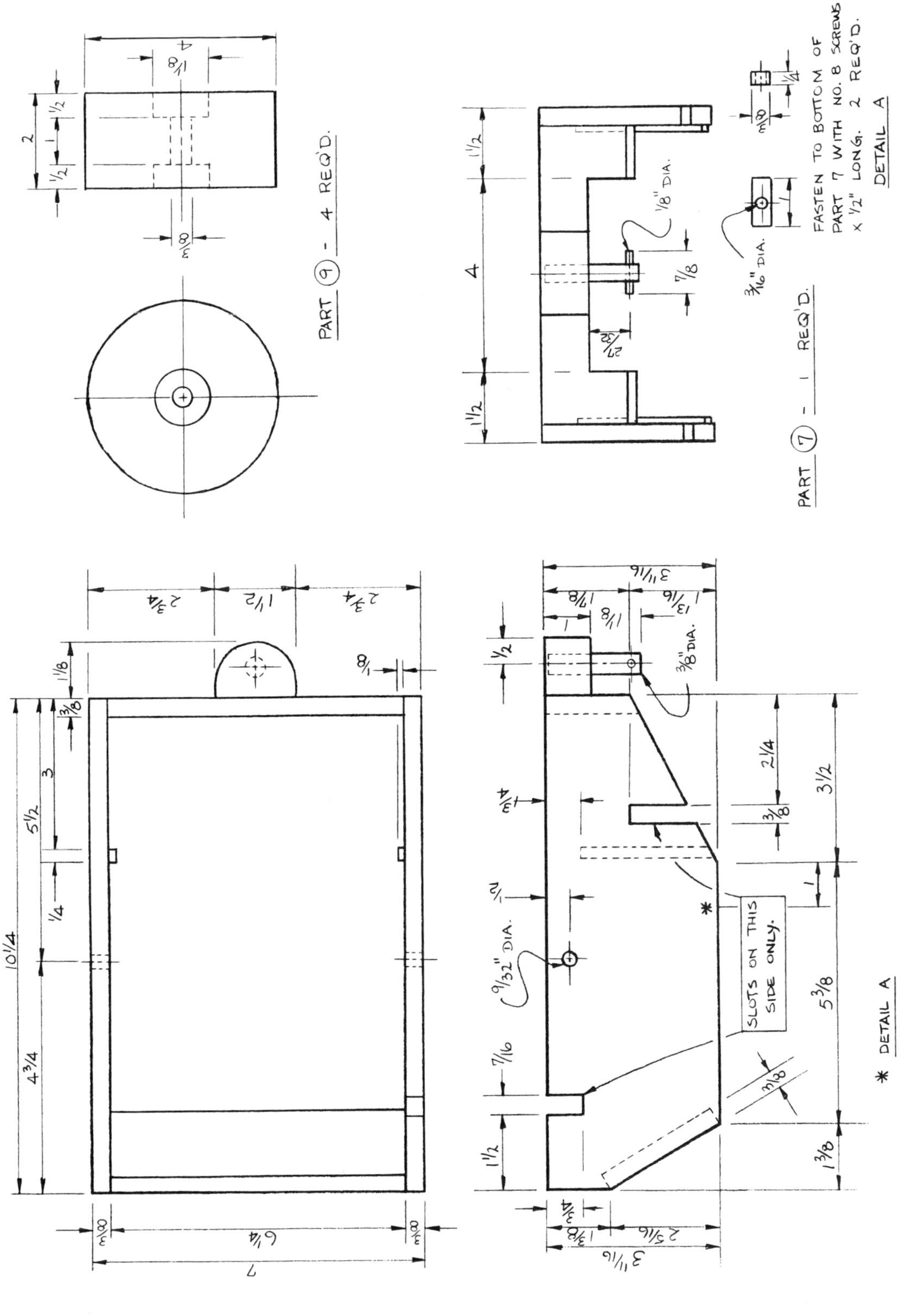
PART 9 - 4 REQ'D.
PART 7 - 1 REQ'D.
1/8" DIA.
3/16" DIA.
FASTEN TO BOTTOM OF PART 7 WITH NO. 8 SCREWS x 1/2" LONG. 2 REQ'D.
DETAIL A
3/8" DIA.
9/32" DIA.
SLOTS ON THIS SIDE ONLY.
* DETAIL A

Illus. 53

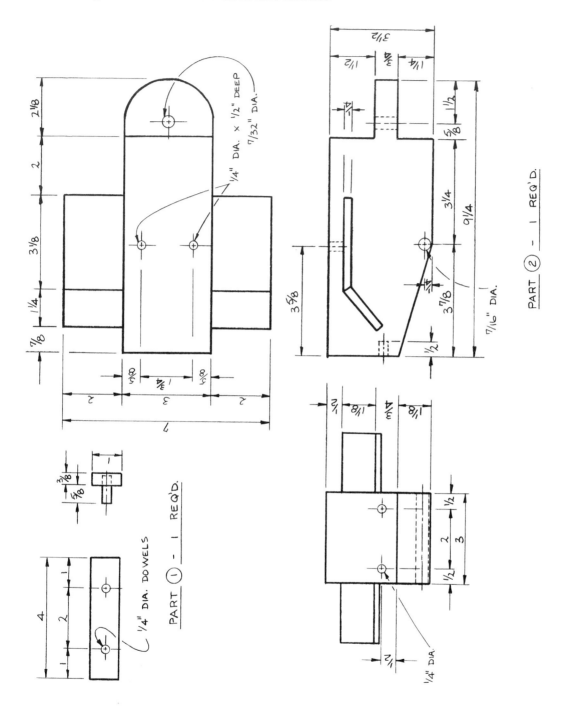

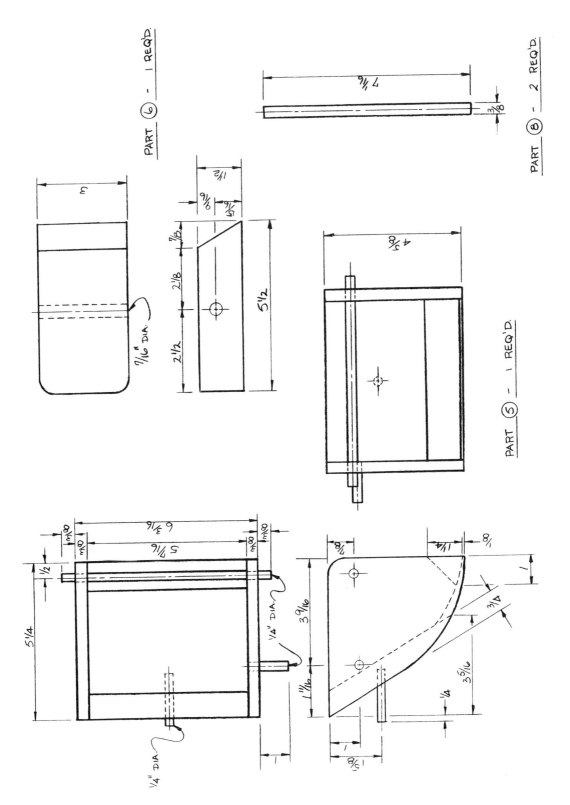

PART 6 - 1 REQ'D.

PART 8 - 2 REQ'D.

PART 5 - 1 REQ'D.

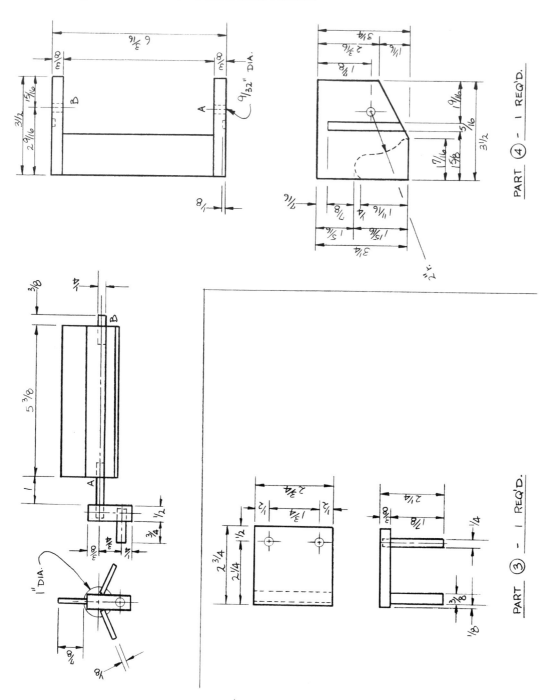

PART ④ – 1 REQ'D.

PART ③ – 1 REQ'D.

ROAD PACKER

Illus. 57. Road packer

1. Start with part 4. Shape to specified dimensions. Drill all holes.

2. Install part 3 to part 4.

3. Shape part 5 to specified dimensions.

4. Fasten part 6 to part 5.

5. Install parts 1, 2, and 7.

6. Connect part 4 to part 5 with part 8. Make sure parts 4 and 5 pivot freely.

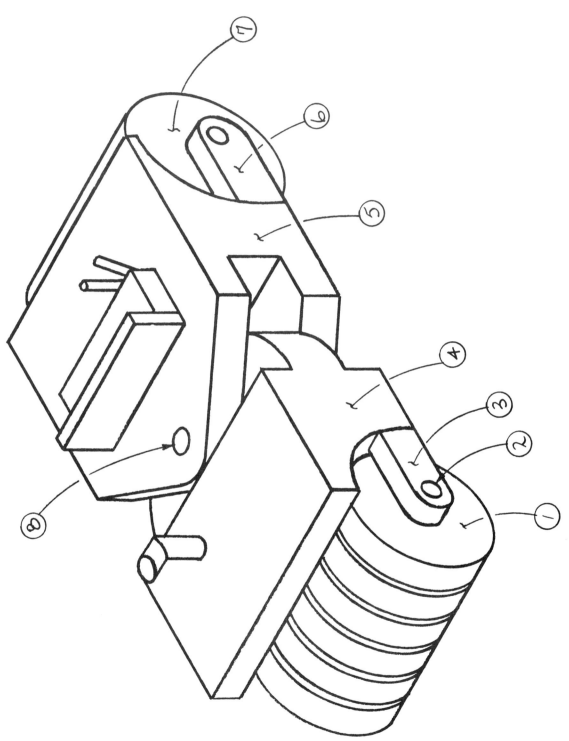

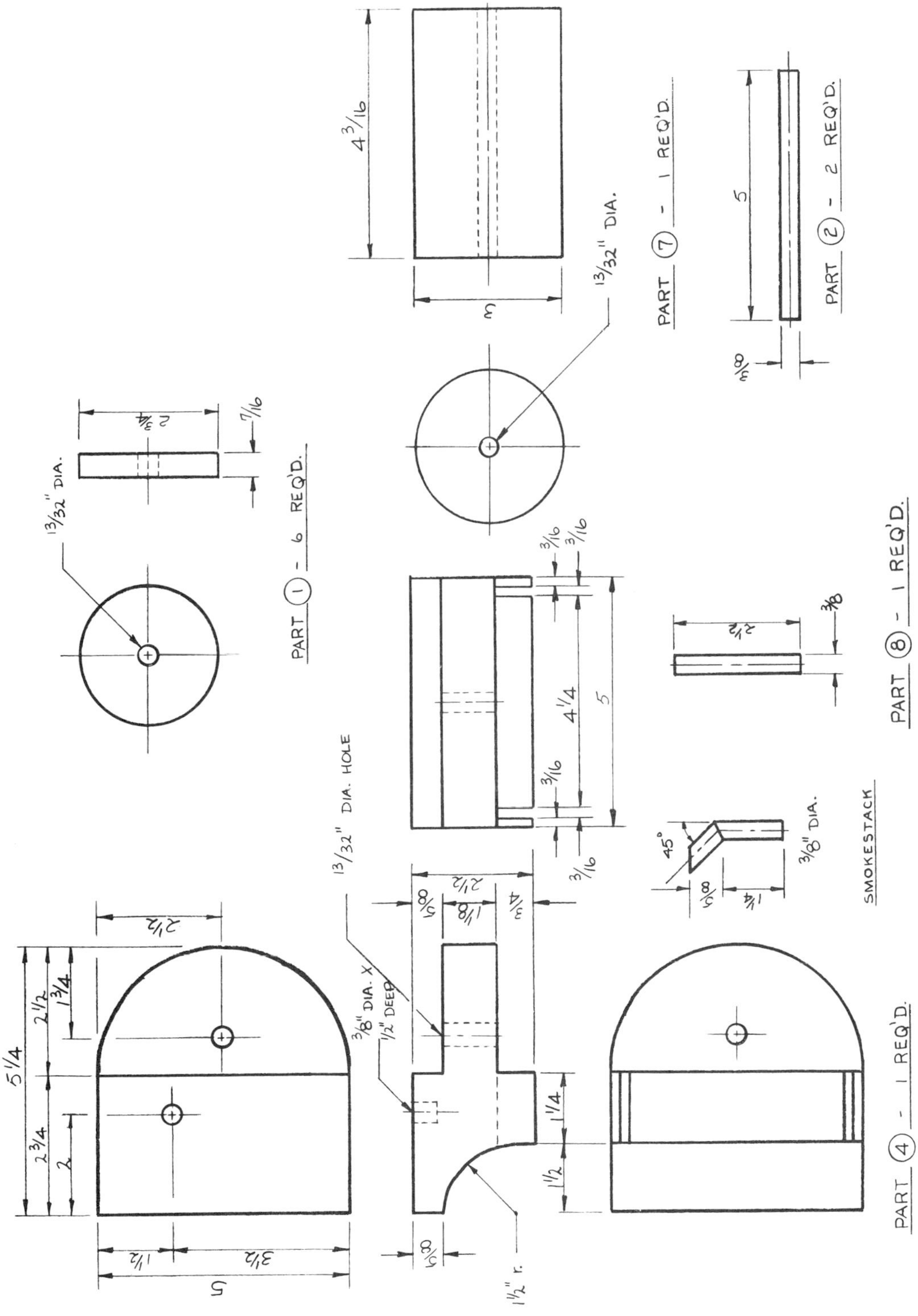

PART ⑦ – 1 REQ'D.

$4^3/16$

3

$13/32$" DIA.

PART ② – 2 REQ'D.

5

$3/8$

PART ① – 6 REQ'D.

$2^3/4$

$7/16$

$13/32$" DIA.

PART ⑧ – 1 REQ'D.

$2^1/2$

$3/8$

SMOKESTACK

$3/8$" DIA.

45°

$5/8$

$1^1/4$

$3/16$ $3/16$

5

$4^1/4$

$3/16$

$3/16$

$13/32$" DIA. HOLE

PART ④ – 1 REQ'D.

$2^1/2$

$3/4$

$2^1/2$

$5^1/4$

$2^3/4$

2

$1^1/2$

$3^1/2$

5

$5/8$

$1^1/8$

$2^1/2$

$3/4$

$3/8$" DIA. X
$1/2$" DEEP

$1^1/4$

$1^1/2$

$5/8$

$1^1/2$" r.

Illus. 59

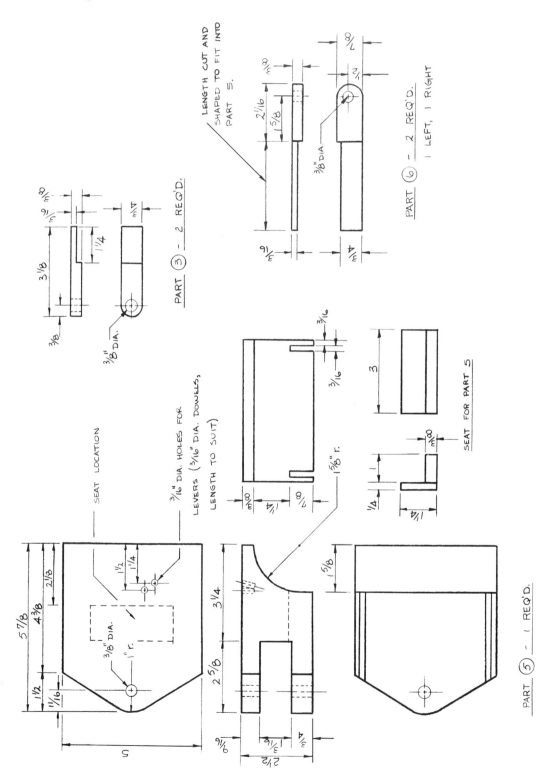

Illus. 60

GRADER

Illus. 61. Grader

1. Start with part 2. Assemble all components, making sure all pieces move freely. Install front wheels.

2. Complete part 9. Cut dadoes and drill all holes as indicated. Fit front wheel assembly to chassis after material has been removed to allow steering clearance. Fasten wheel assembly to part 9 with screws or dowels.

3. Assemble part 6 and install. When everything is working to your satisfaction, fill in the remainder of the dado, allowing room for steering dowels to move freely.

4. Install remaining parts 1 and 4.

5. Install parts 3 and 8. As the top of part 8 is pushed down, the blade assembly should rise.

6. Install parts 5 and 7.

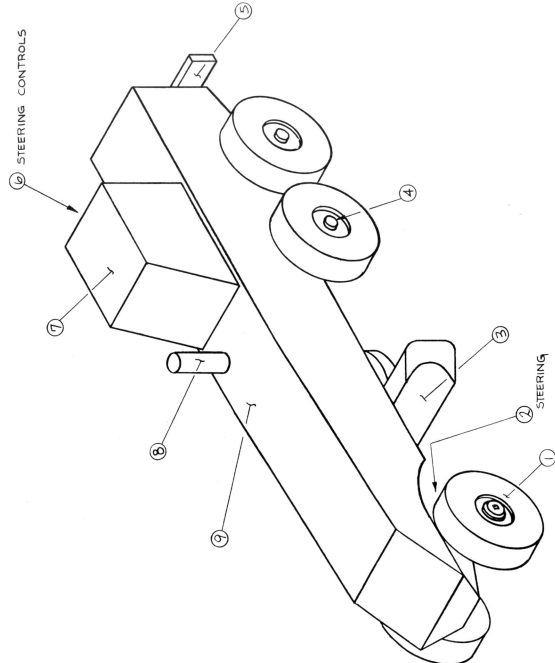

STEERING CONTROLS

STEERING

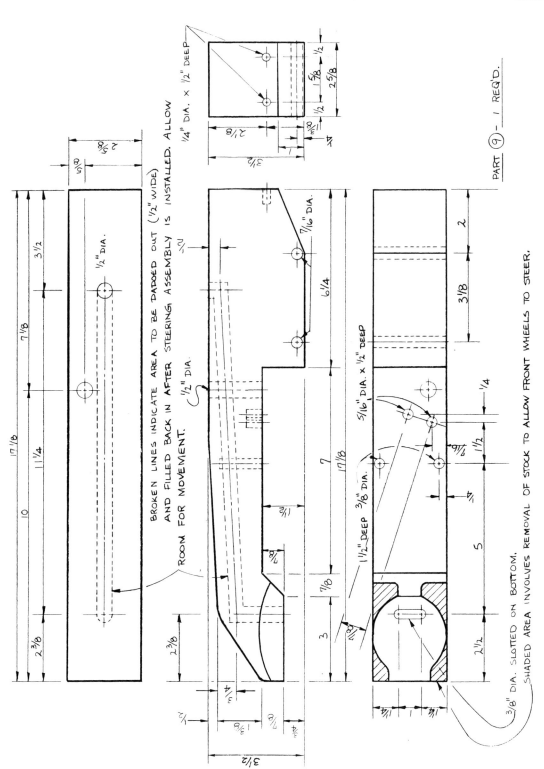

PART ⑨ - 1 REQ'D.

BROKEN LINES INDICATE AREA TO BE DADOED OUT (½" WIDE) AND FILLED BACK IN AFTER STEERING ASSEMBLY IS INSTALLED. ALLOW ROOM FOR MOVEMENT.

3/8" DIA. SLOTTED ON BOTTOM. SHADED AREA INVOLVES REMOVAL OF STOCK TO ALLOW FRONT WHEELS TO STEER.

Illus. 63

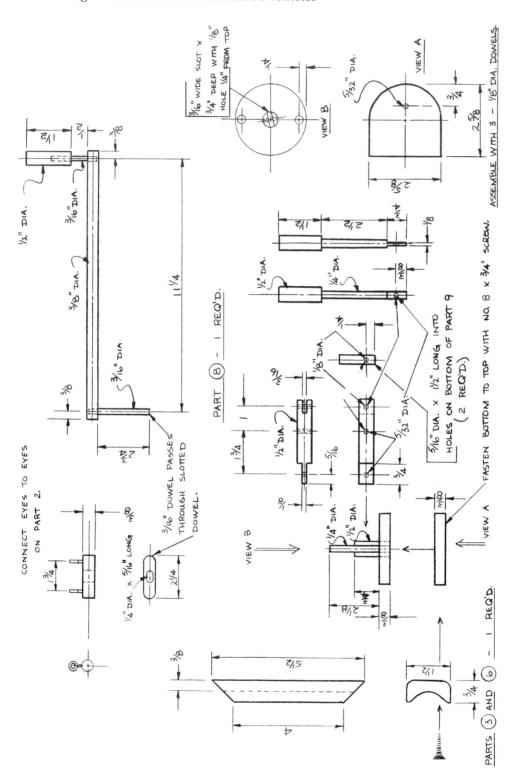

Illus. 64

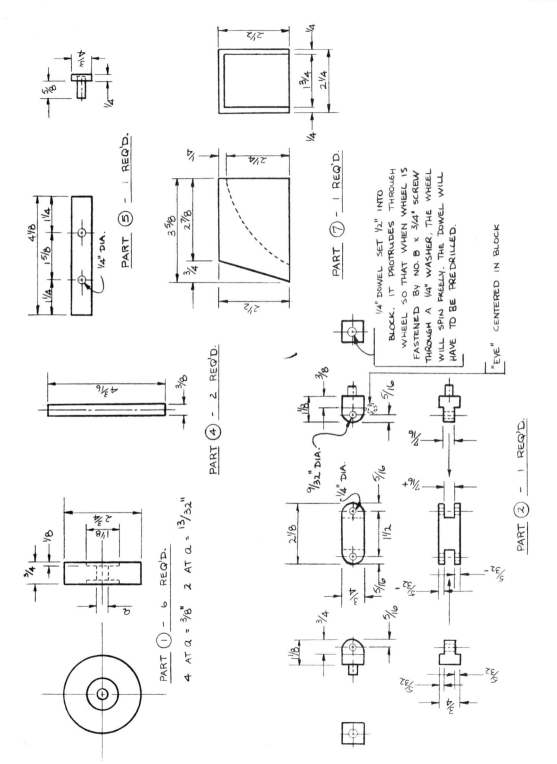

PART (5) - 1 REQ'D.

1/4" DIA.

PART (7) - 1 REQ'D.

PART (4) - 2 REQ'D.

1/4" DOWEL SET 1/2" INTO BLOCK. IT PROTRUDES THROUGH WHEEL SO THAT WHEN WHEEL IS FASTENED BY NO. 8 x 3/4" SCREW THROUGH A 1/4" WASHER, THE WHEEL WILL SPIN FREELY. THE DOWEL WILL HAVE TO BE PREDRILLED.

"EYE" CENTERED IN BLOCK

9/32 DIA.

1/4" DIA.

PART (2) - 1 REQ'D.

PART (1) - 6 REQ'D.

4 AT a = 3/8"   2 AT a = 13/32"

LOG LOADER

Illus. 66. Log loader

1. Start with part 3. Shape as specified. Drill all holes.

2. Cut part 4 to specified dimensions and shape. Drill all holes.

3. Connect part 3 to part 4 with ⅜"-diameter dowel that is 2½" long.

4. Laminate part 1 to part 4 and then part 2 to part 3.

5. Install parts 5 and 6.

6. Assemble parts 7, 8, 9, 10, 11, 12, 13, 14, 15, 16, 17, 18, 19, 20, and 21, as indicated by blueprints and plan view of grapple (see Illus. 71). Make sure levers can move freely.

7. Part 16 is fastened to part 15 and part 17 is fastened to part 18 with a ½"-long #8 screw.

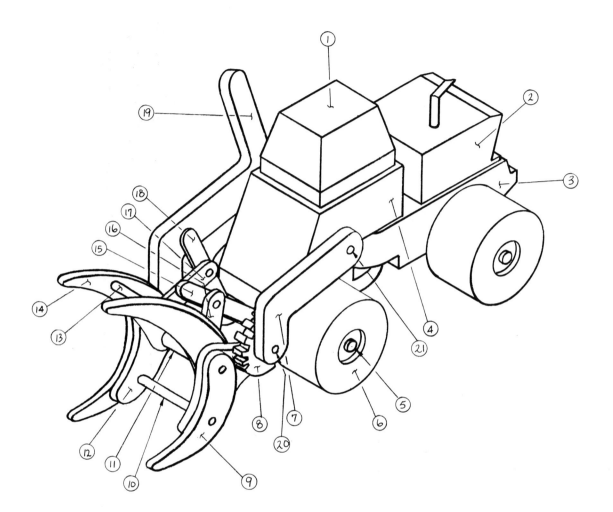

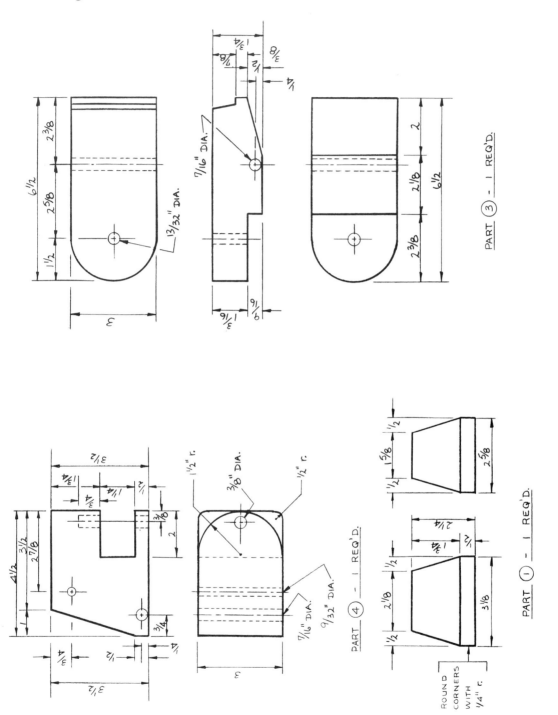

Illus. 68

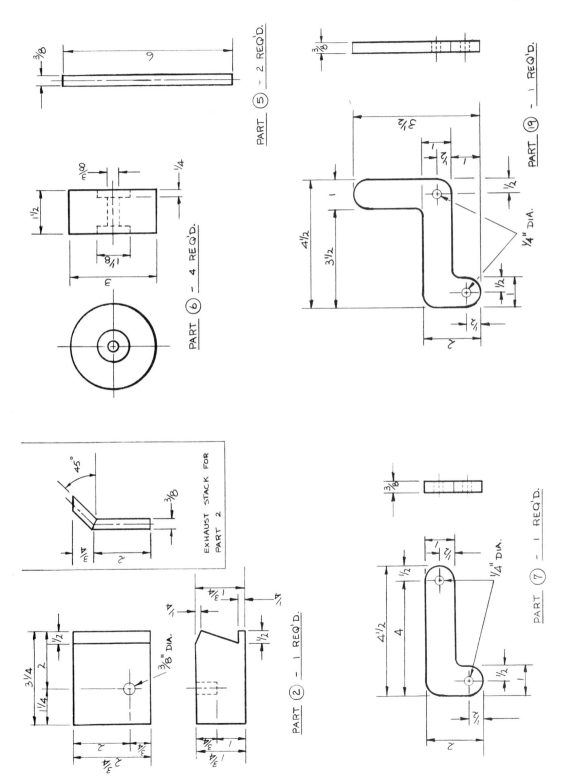

PART ⑤ — 2 REQ'D.

PART ⑥ — 4 REQ'D.

PART ⑨ — 1 REQ'D.

¼" DIA.

EXHAUST STACK FOR PART 2

PART ② — 1 REQ'D.

⅜" DIA.

PART ⑦ — 1 REQ'D.

¼" DIA.

Illus. 69

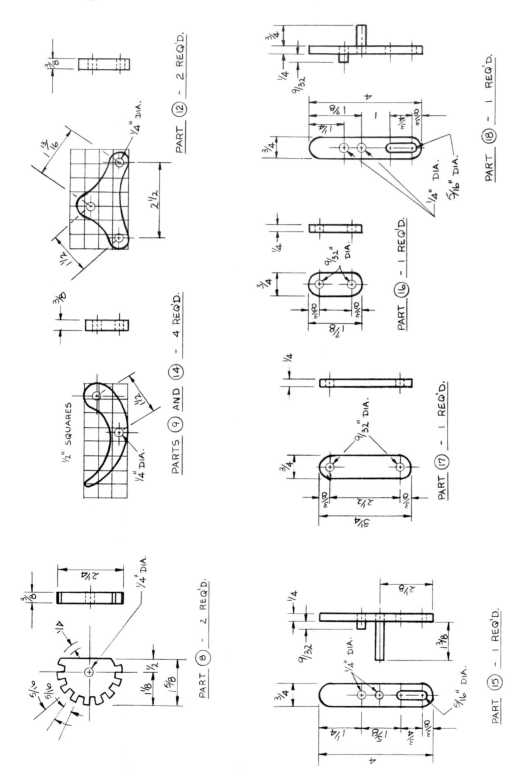

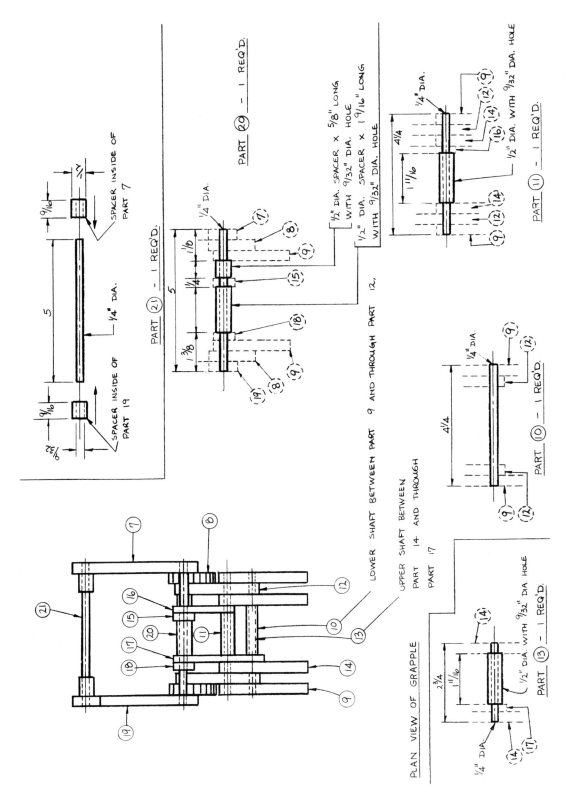

PLAN VIEW OF GRAPPLE

Illus. 71

LOGGING TRUCK—CAB

Illus. 72. Logging truck—cab

1. Start with part 11. It is made in three separate layers laminated together. Shape each piece to specified dimensions before gluing together. Drill all holes.

2. Fasten part 6 to part 10. Glue assembly into position on part 11.

3. Install remaining parts in this order: 2 and 3, 1, 4, 5, 7, 8, and 9.

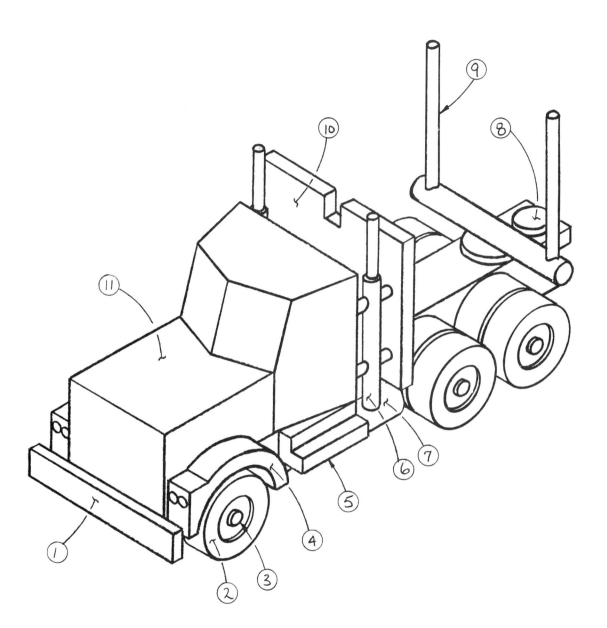

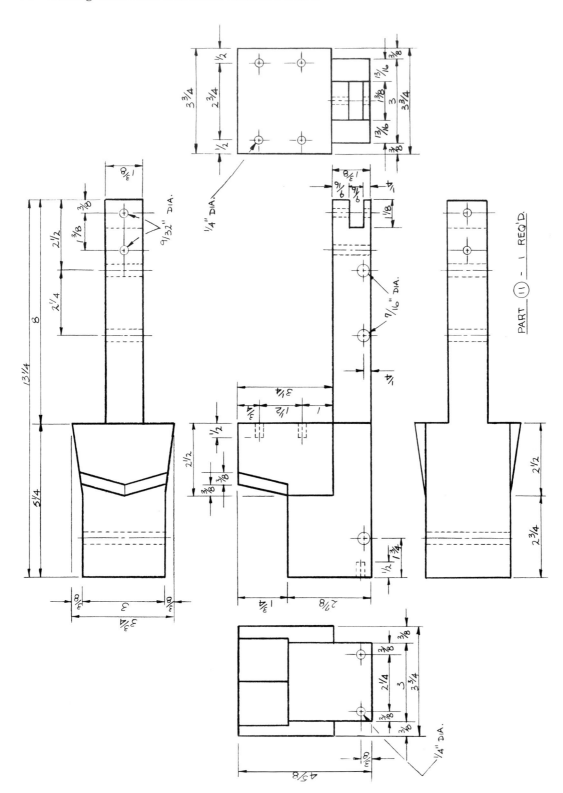

PART (11) - 1 REQ'D.

Illus. 74

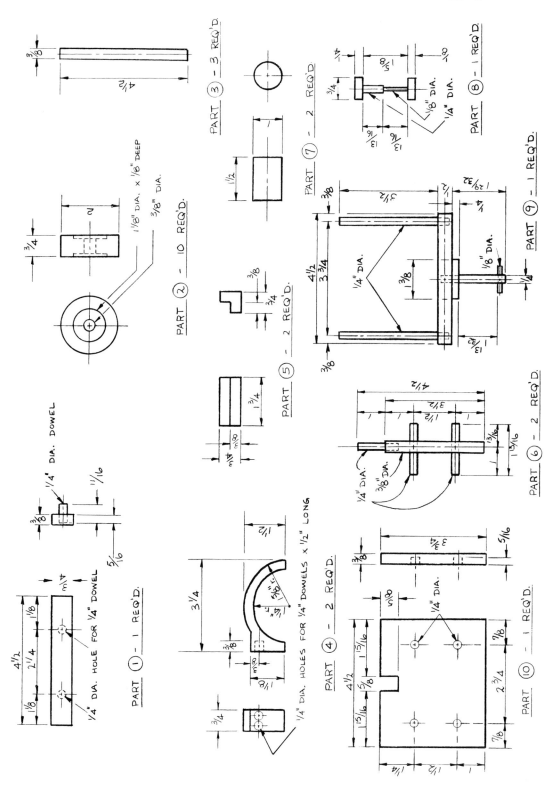

LOGGING TRUCK—TRAILER

Illus. 76. Logging truck—trailer

1. Start with part 1. Drill all holes.

2. Install parts 2, 3, and 4.

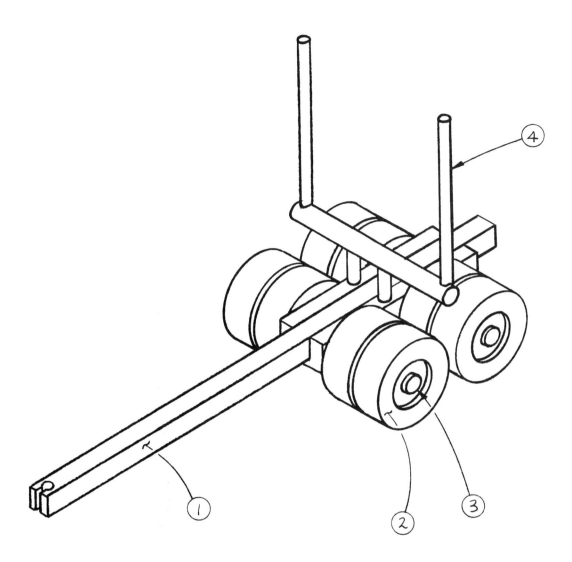

Illus. 77

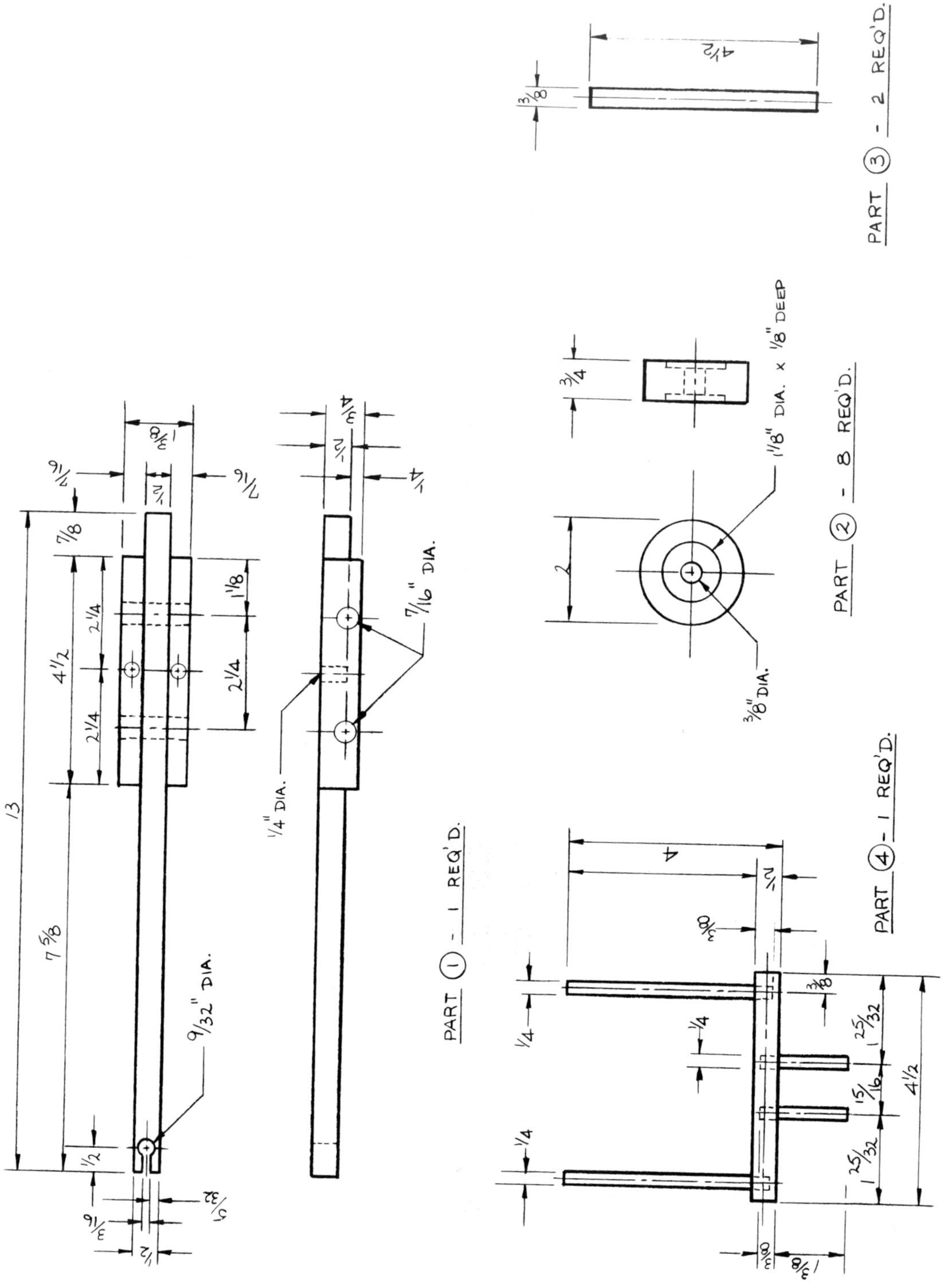

PART ③ - 2 REQ'D.

PART ② - 8 REQ'D.

1⅛" DIA. × ⅛" DEEP

⅜ DIA.

PART ① - 1 REQ'D.

¼" DIA.

7/16" DIA.

9/32" DIA.

PART ④ - 1 REQ'D.

Illus. 78

TRACTOR

Illus. 79. Tractor

1. Start with part 10. Cut and shape to specified dimensions. Drill all holes.

2. Assemble part 2 along with front wheels (part 3). Connect assembly to part 10 with screws or dowels.

3. Install parts 13 and 4. Then install part 1.

4. Install part 11. Make sure steering assembly turns freely as you rotate the steering wheel.

5. Assemble part 8. Install parts 6, 9, 8, 5, 7, and 12.

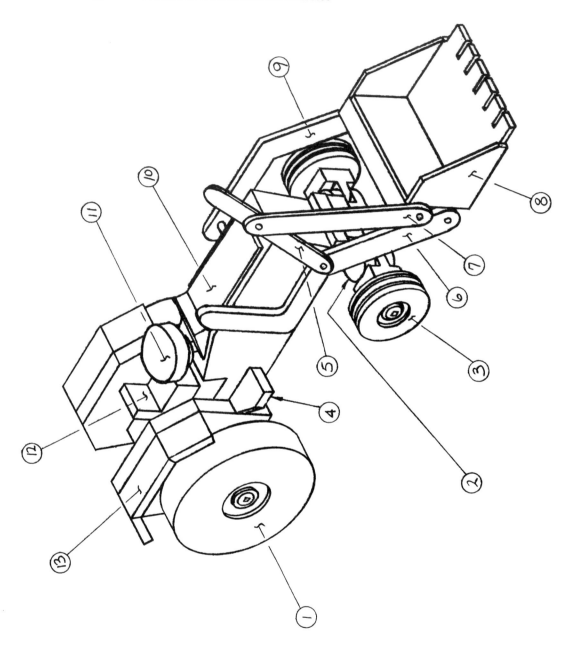

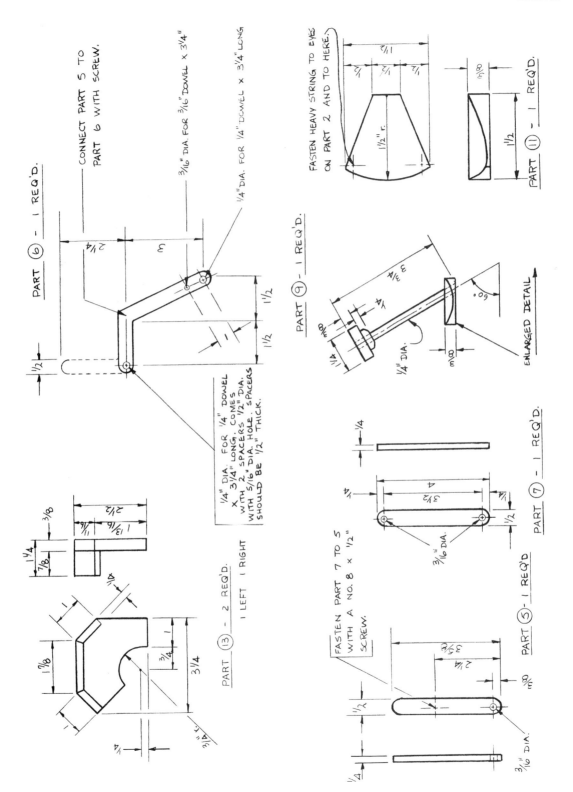

CONNECT PART 5 TO PART 6 WITH SCREW.

3/16" DIA. FOR 3/16" DOWEL × 3/4".

1/4" DIA. FOR 1/4" DOWEL × 3/4" LONG

PART 6 - 1 REQ'D.

2 1/4

3

1/2

1 1/2

1 1/2

1

1/4" DIA. FOR 1/4" DOWEL × 3/4" LONG. COMES WITH 2 SPACERS 1/2" DIA. WITH 5/16" DIA. HOLE. SPACERS SHOULD BE 1/2" THICK.

FASTEN HEAVY STRING TO EYES ON PART 2 AND TO HERE.

1/7

1/4 1/4 1/4

1 1/2" r.

9/8

1 1/2

PART 11 - 1 REQ'D.

PART 9 - 1 REQ'D.

3/8

3/4

1/4

1/4 DIA.

3/8

60°

ENLARGED DETAIL

3/8

1 13/16

2 1/2

1 1/4

7/8

1/4

1

1

3/4

3/4

1 7/8

1/4

3/4"

1

PART 13 - 2 REQ'D.
1 LEFT 1 RIGHT

1/4

3 1/2

4

1/4

1/2

3/16" DIA.

PART 7 - 1 REQ'D

FASTEN PART 7 TO 5 WITH A NO. 8 × 1/2" SCREW.

PART 5 - 1 REQ'D

3 5/8

2 1/4

3/8

1

1/2

3/16" DIA.

1/4

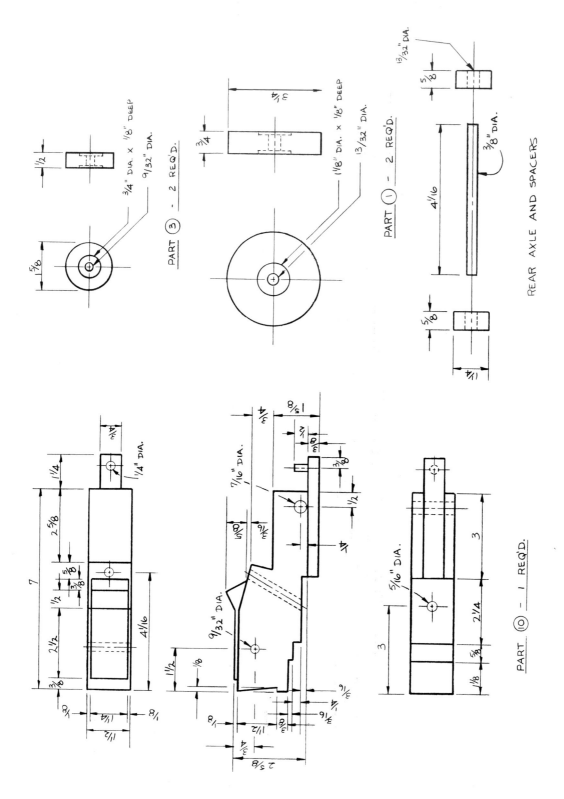

PART ③ - 2 REQ'D.

3/4" DIA. × 1/8" DEEP

9/32" DIA.

1/2

5/8

3/4

3 1/4

1 1/8" DIA. × 1/8" DEEP

13/32" DIA.

PART ① - 2 REQ'D.

13/32" DIA.

3/8" DIA.

5/8

5/8

4 1/16

1 1/4

REAR AXLE AND SPACERS

7

1 1/4

2 5/8

5/8

3/8

1/2

2 1/2

3/8

1/4" DIA.

4 1/16

5/8

1 1/4

1/8

1 1/2

7/16" DIA.

9/32" DIA.

3/4

1 5/8

1/2

3/8

3/8

1/2

5/8

5/8

1/4

1 1/2

1/8

1 1/2

3/8

3/16

1/4

3/16

3/4

2 5/8

5/16" DIA.

3

3

2 1/4

5/8

1/8

PART ⑩ - 1 REQ'D.

Illus. 82

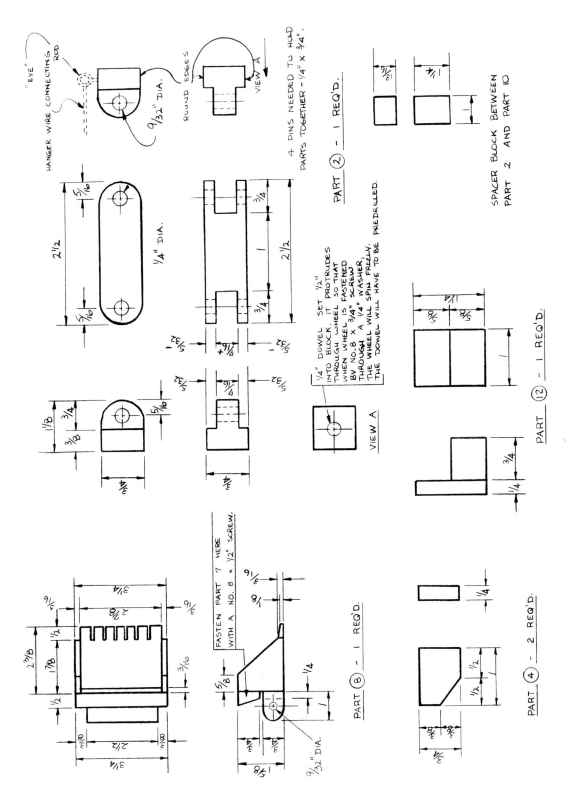

"EYE"

HANGER WIRE CONNECTING ROD

ROUND EDGES

VIEW A

$\frac{9}{32}$" DIA.

4 PINS NEEDED TO HOLD PARTS TOGETHER - $\frac{1}{4}$" X $\frac{3}{4}$".

PART 2 - 1 REQ'D.

SPACER BLOCK BETWEEN PART 2 AND PART 10

$2\frac{1}{2}$

$\frac{5}{16}$

$\frac{5}{16}$

$\frac{1}{4}$" DIA.

$\frac{3}{4}$

$\frac{3}{4}$

$2\frac{1}{2}$

$\frac{5}{32}$

$+\frac{1}{16}$

$\frac{5}{32}$

$1\frac{3}{16}$

$1\frac{1}{4}$

1

$\frac{1}{4}$" DOWEL SET $\frac{1}{2}$" INTO BLOCK. IT PROTRUDES THROUGH WHEEL SO THAT WHEN WHEEL IS FASTENED BY NO. 8 X $\frac{3}{4}$" SCREW THROUGH A $\frac{1}{4}$" WASHER, THE WHEEL WILL SPIN FREELY. THE DOWEL WILL HAVE TO BE PREDRILLED.

VIEW A

$1\frac{1}{8}$

$\frac{3}{4}$

$\frac{3}{8}$

$\frac{5}{16}$

$\frac{5}{32}$

$\frac{3}{4}$

$\frac{9}{16}$

$\frac{1}{4}$

$\frac{5}{32}$

$\frac{3}{4}$

$\frac{1}{4}$

$\frac{3}{8}$

$\frac{5}{8}$

1

$\frac{3}{4}$

$\frac{3}{4}$

PART 12 - 1 REQ'D.

$3\frac{1}{4}$

$\frac{3}{16}$

$2\frac{1}{8}$

$\frac{3}{16}$

$\frac{1}{2}$

$2\frac{3}{8}$

$1\frac{7}{8}$

$\frac{3}{16}$

$\frac{1}{2}$

$\frac{3}{8}$

$2\frac{1}{2}$

$\frac{3}{8}$

$3\frac{1}{4}$

FASTEN PART 7 HERE WITH A NO. 8 × $\frac{1}{2}$" SCREW.

$\frac{3}{16}$

$\frac{1}{8}$

$\frac{5}{8}$

$\frac{1}{4}$

1

$\frac{3}{4}$

$\frac{3}{4}$

$1\frac{5}{8}$

$\frac{9}{32}$" DIA.

PART 8 - 1 REQ'D.

$\frac{1}{4}$

$\frac{1}{2}$

$\frac{1}{2}$

1

$\frac{3}{8}$

$\frac{3}{8}$

$\frac{3}{4}$

PART 4 - 2 REQ'D.

Illus. 83

LUMBER TRUCK

Illus. 84. Lumber truck

1. Start with part 10. Cut to specified shape. Drill all holes.

2. Glue part 12 to part 10.

3. Install parts 2 and 3.

4. Assemble parts 6, 8, and 9. Glue assembly onto part 12.

5. Install parts 4, 5, 1, 11, and 7.

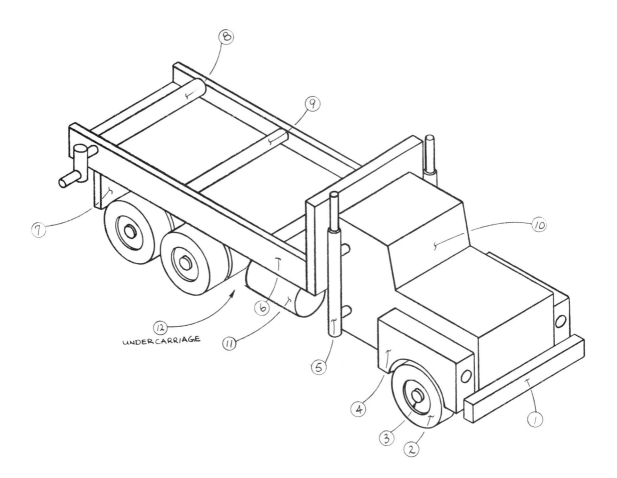

UNDERCARRIAGE

Illus. 85

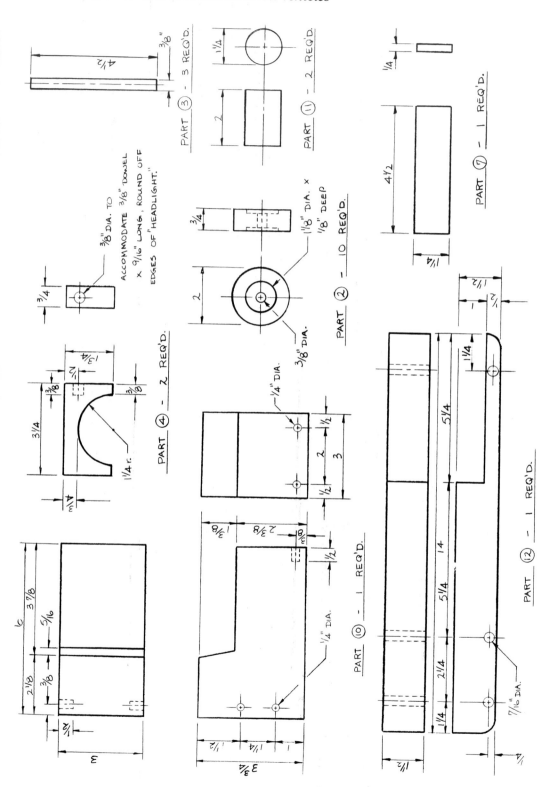

Illus. 86

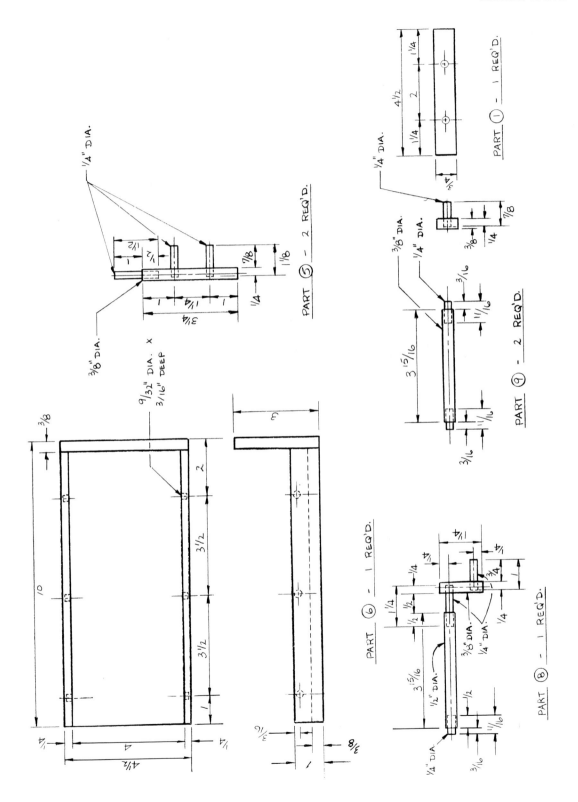

PART ① - 1 REQ'D.

PART ⑤ - 2 REQ'D.

PART ⑥ - 1 REQ'D.

PART ⑧ - 1 REQ'D.

PART ⑨ - 2 REQ'D.

BULLDOZER

Illus. 88. Bulldozer

1. Start with part 2. Shape to specified dimensions.

2. Assemble parts 7 and 11.

3. Dry-fit parts 8, 9, and 10. Stretch out treads to determine final location for rear axle hole in part 2. (See Illus. 90.)

4. Drill all holes in part 2.

5. Assemble parts 8, 9, and 10 along with treads.

6. Install part 12.

7. Install remaining parts in this order: 1, 6, 5, 4, and 3.

Note: Treads are delicate in installation stages when you are pinning them together with tin connecting links (part 11). Therefore, make more of part 7 than needed in case any should break during installation.

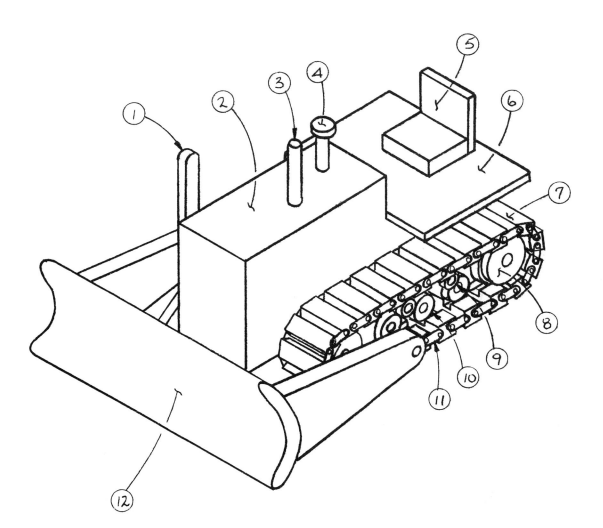

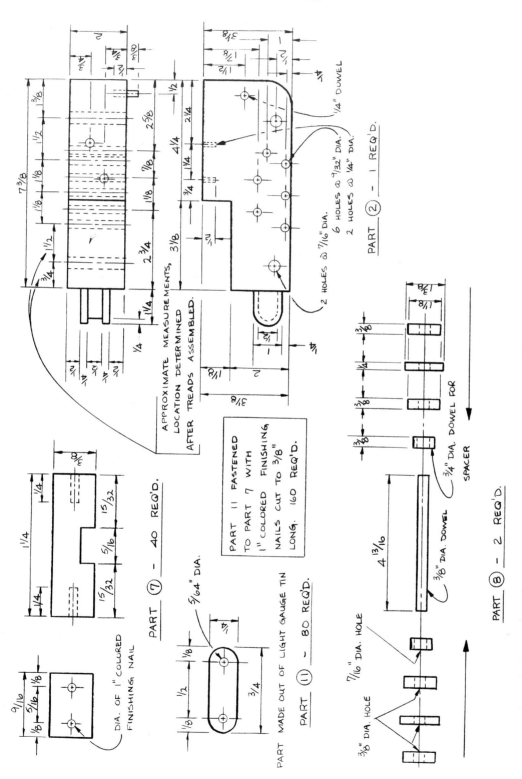

APPROXIMATE MEASUREMENTS, LOCATION DETERMINED AFTER TREADS ASSEMBLED.

PART ② — 1 REQ'D.

6 HOLES @ 9/32" DIA.
2 HOLES @ 1/4" DIA.

1/4" DOWEL

2 HOLES @ 7/16" DIA.

PART ⑦ — 40 REQ'D.

PART 11 FASTENED TO PART 7 WITH 1" COLORED FINISHING NAILS CUT TO 3/8" LONG. 160 REQ'D.

DIA. OF 1" COLORED FINISHING NAIL.

5/64" DIA.

PART ⑪ — 80 REQ'D.

PART MADE OUT OF LIGHT GAUGE TIN

3/4" DIA. DOWEL FOR SPACER

3/8" DIA. DOWEL

7/16" DIA. HOLE

3/8" DIA. HOLE

PART ⑧ — 2 REQ'D.

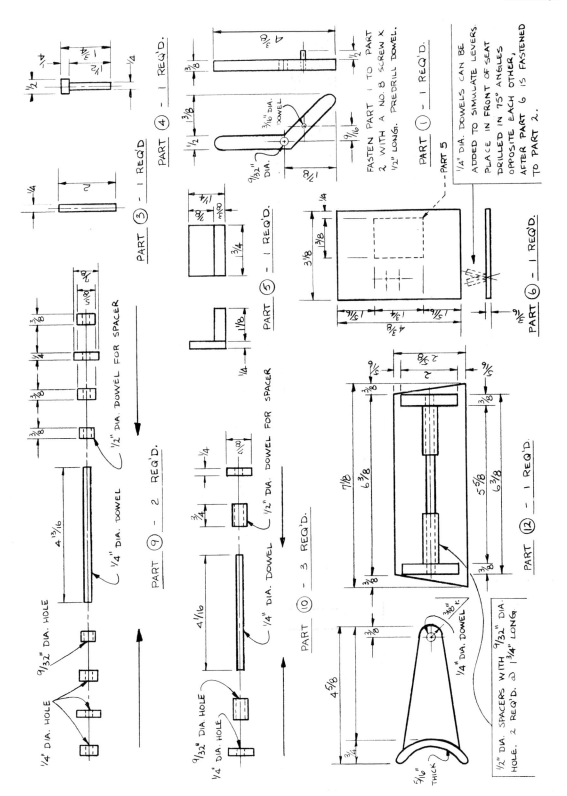

FASTEN PART 1 TO PART 2 WITH A NO. 8 SCREW X 1/2" LONG. PREDRILL DOWEL.

PART ① - 1 REQ'D.

1/4" DIA. DOWELS CAN BE ADDED TO SIMULATE LEVERS. PLACE IN FRONT OF SEAT DRILLED IN 75° ANGLES OPPOSITE EACH OTHER, AFTER PART 6 IS FASTENED TO PART 2.

PART ③ - 1 REQ'D

PART ④ - 1 REQ'D.

3/16" DIA. DOWEL

9/32" DIA.

PART ⑤ - 1 REQ'D.

PART 5

PART ⑥ - 1 REQ'D.

PART ⑨ - 2 REQ'D.

1/2" DIA. DOWEL FOR SPACER

1/4" DIA. DOWEL

9/32" DIA. HOLE

1/4" DIA. HOLE

PART ⑩ - 3 REQ'D.

1/2" DIA. DOWEL FOR SPACER

1/4" DIA. DOWEL

9/32" DIA. HOLE

1/4" DIA. HOLE

PART ⑫ - 1 REQ'D.

1/4" DIA. DOWEL

1/2" DIA. SPACERS WITH 9/32" DIA. HOLE. 2 REQ'D. @ 1 3/4" LONG.

3/8" r.

5/16" THICK

Illus. 91

LOW-BED TRAILER

Illus. 92. Low-bed trailer

1. Start with part 2. You should fasten the front two pieces by the hitch pin to the main body with plugged screws or dowels. Drill all holes.

2. Install hitch pin (part 1), part 3, and part 4.

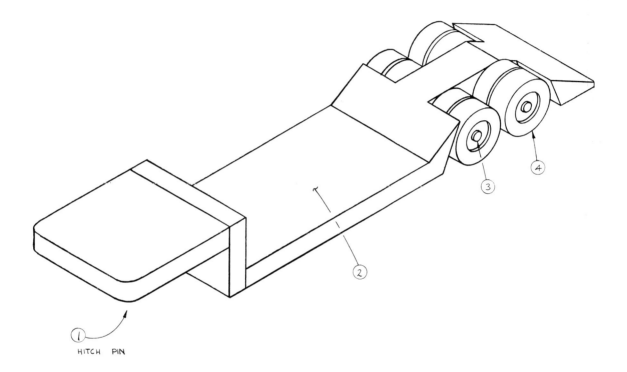

HITCH PIN

Illus. 93

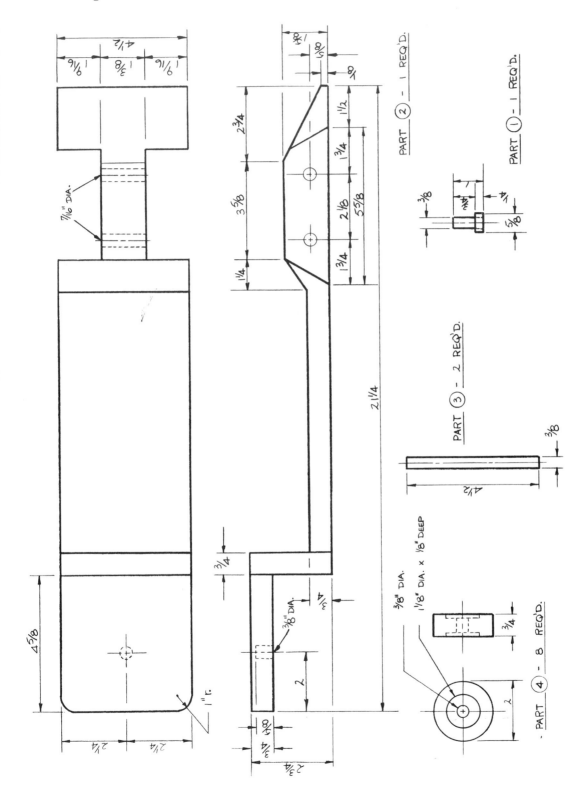

PART ② – 1 REQ'D.

PART ① – 1 REQ'D.

PART ③ – 2 REQ'D.

PART ④ – 8 REQ'D.

Illus. 94

CEMENT MIXER

Illus. 95. Cement mixer

1. Start with part 13. Make it out of three laminations that are 1½", 1½", and 1¼". Drill all holes and cut the dado for the chassis (see Illus. 98).

2. Shape part 2 as shown. Drill axle holes. Install part 7 to part 2. Install whole assembly into dado on part 13.

3. Install parts 4, 5, 3, 11, 12, 20, 9, 6, and 14.

4. Turn the drum portion of part 16 on a lathe. Now comes the hard part: hollowing out the drum. The way I did this step (you may think of another way) was to split the drum on a bandsaw; then I

hollowed out the two halves, according to dimensions, using an electric gouge. Once hollowed out, fluting has to be installed. I used ½" × ¹⁄₁₆" oak strips. Make saw kerfs that are ³⁄₈" deep and ¼" apart. This will permit the strips to conform to the inside shape of the drum. Install using a hot-melt glue gun and then fill all the kerfs with glue to add stability and strength. Fit the two halves of the drum together and make sure that the fluting lines up on the joint. Glue together. Install the rest of the drum assembly.

5. Install parts 16, 17, and 8 simultaneously. Adjust position of part 8 so that drum spins freely but is still locked into proper position on part 17. Be sure to install rubber band or elastic ring to drum before final installation to part 8.

6. Install part 10 and, at the same time, slip the elastic ring onto the crank pulley. Crank should now spin the drum.

7. Install part 15.

8. Shape and install part 18.

9. Install parts 19 and 1. There should be enough clearance between the two that a marble can roll down the discharge chute when pivoted in any direction.

Note: Additional chutes can be made and stored between parts 6 and 17. Use ¹⁄₈"-diameter dowels to connect chutes.

WATER TANK

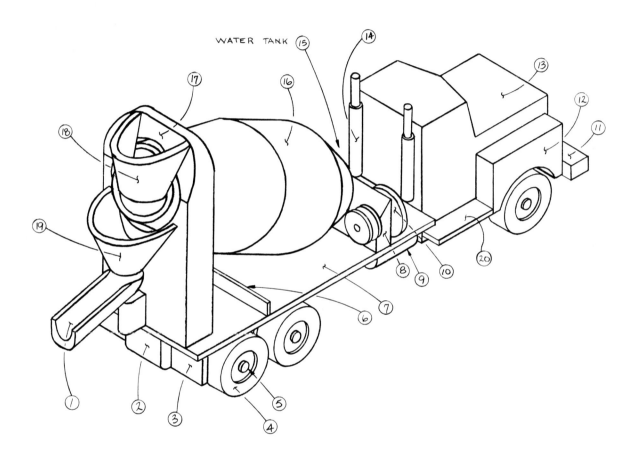

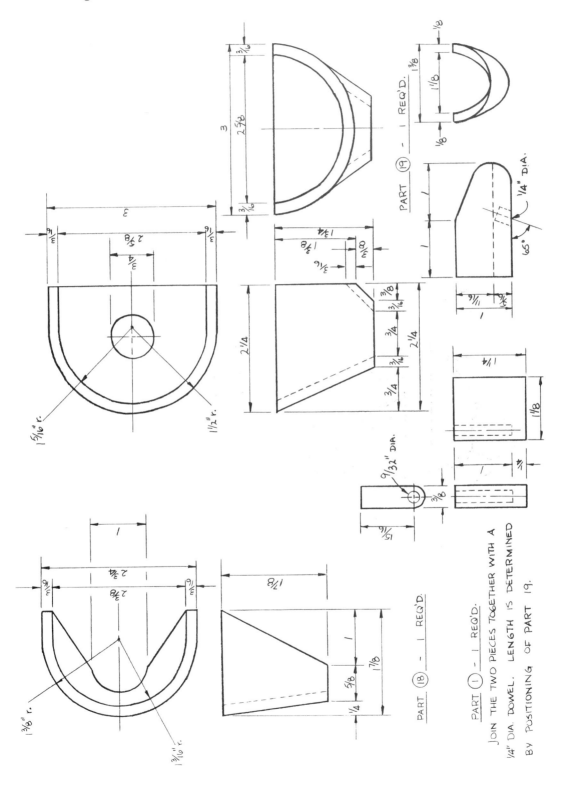

PART ⑲ — 1 REQ'D.

PART ⑱ — 1 REQ'D.

PART ① — 1 REQ'D.
JOIN THE TWO PIECES TOGETHER WITH A
¼" DIA. DOWEL. LENGTH IS DETERMINED
BY POSITIONING OF PART 19.

Illus. 97

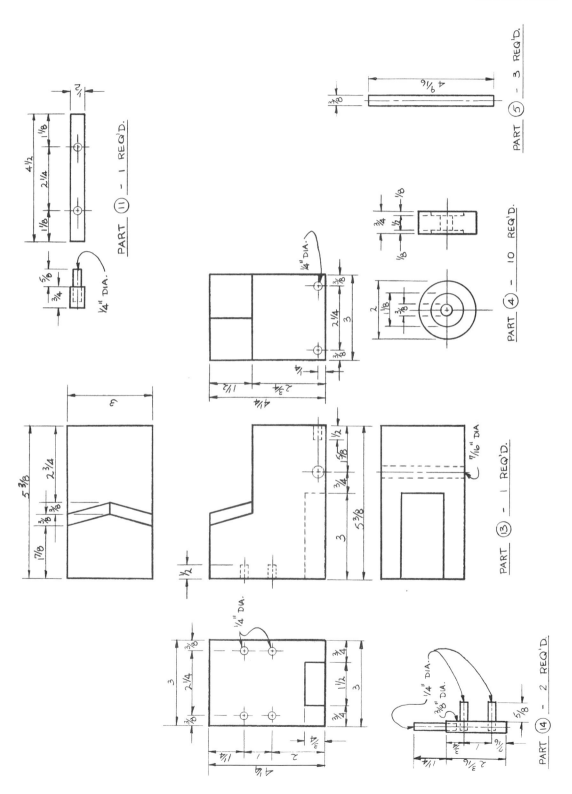

PART (11) – I REQ'D.

PART (5) – 3 REQ'D.

PART (4) – 10 REQ'D.

PART (13) – I REQ'D.

PART (14) – 2 REQ'D.

Illus. 98

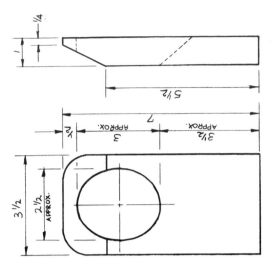

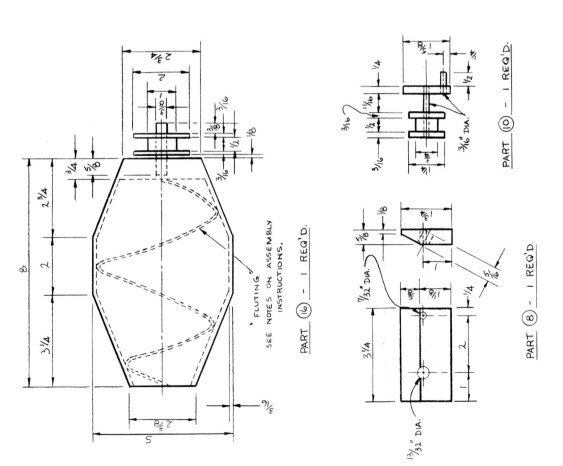

DRUM SUPPORT HOLE TO BE CONTOURED TO MATCH FINISHED DRUM. HOLE DIMENSIONS ARE APPROXIMATE. CHECK FOR FIT WITH DRUM BEFORE INSTALLING. WAX INSIDE EDGE OF HOLE SO THAT DRUM WILL TURN FREELY.

PART ⑰ - 1 REQ'D.

"FLUTING"
SEE NOTES ON ASSEMBLY
INSTRUCTIONS.

PART ⑯ - 1 REQ'D.

PART ⑩ - 1 REQ'D.

PART ⑧ - 1 REQ'D.

Illus. 99

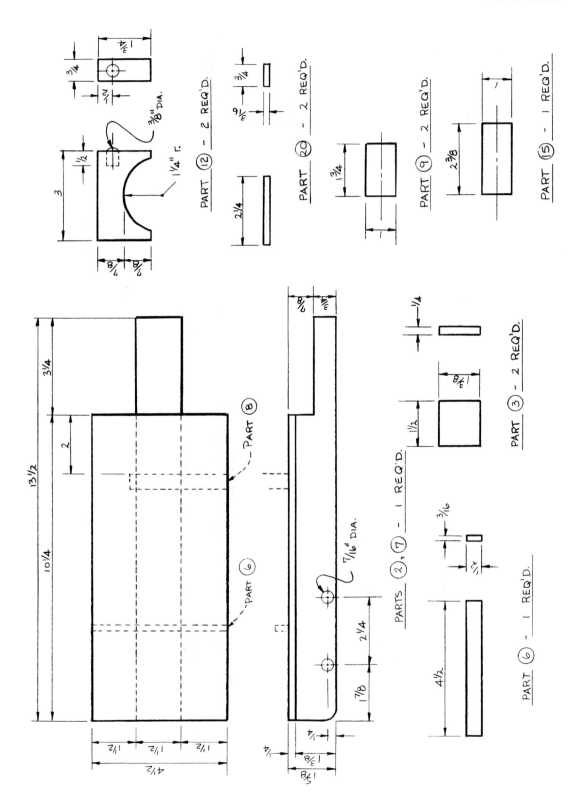

CRANE

Illus. 101. Crane

1. Start with part 7. Cut main block to indicated size and shape (18½″ × 4½″ × 1⅝″). Drill holes for outriggers (see Illus. 112). Cut dado through bottom of block where outriggers slide. Block in part of dado to serve as stops for outriggers. Once you've installed the outriggers, these stops will prevent them from falling out. Drill slots for steering assembly. Drill holes for turntable assembly (the perimeter holes are designed to accept standard-sized marbles to act as bearings). Drill axle holes in chassis piece and install to main block. Install cab. Lastly, install railing pieces.

2. Next, put together the four outriggers but leave off the ⅛″-diameter × ⅝″-long dowel pins. Insert outriggers into main block (part 7). Now install dowel pin into underside of outriggers. These pins will run up against the stops as the outrigger is pulled out and prevent removal.

3. Install rear axles and wheels (parts 9 and 10).

4. Construct steering assemblies. The wheels should be able to spin freely and turn right and left smoothly. A second block (¾″ × ¾″ × 2½″) is used to block down the assembly to permit clearance for wheels under main block (part 7) (see Illus. 105). Fasten assemblies to part 7 with screws, keeping the screw eyes pointing to the rear of the crane.

5. Install the connecting rods (part of part 16) (see Illus. 108). Open up the screw eyes and join to the screw eyes on part 4. Close them up again. Drop part 16 (minus the ½"-diameter × 1"-long dowel) through the slots in part 7 and into the slots of the connecting rods. Now install part 17 and place ½"-diameter × 1"-long dowel onto ³⁄₁₆"-diameter shaft of part 16. Steering assemblies should now work smoothly and together when steering lever is pushed in either direction.

6. Fasten part 11 to part 8 in designated location. Now install parts 14 and 6 to part 8. Part 6 should slide freely on part 8 and be governed in amount of travel by dowel in part 14. Leave off the ¼"-diameter × 1"-long dowel on part 8. Install part 8 and then insert ¼" × 1"-long dowel to lock assembly into position (do not forget to place the eight marbles into position needed for the "bearing").

7. Construct part 15 (the main boom). Be sure not to have any excess glue on inside of assembly or the next section of boom will not slide freely.

8. Construct part 2 (intermediate section of boom). Run the dadoes to the ends and fill them back in to required dimensions to act as stops after you've installed part 1 in part 2.

9. Slide part 1 into part 2. Install stops on part 2. Slide part 2 into part 15. Now install the toothed wheel and lock into place with ¼"-diameter shaft and turning wheel. Be sure that as you rotate the wheel, first the jib slides out and then the intermediate section of boom. It should operate smoothly. You can use ⅛"-diameter × 1"-long dowel to lock the jib into full-out position by installing it in the designated hole on part 2. You should fasten the dowel to top or side of part 2 with a short string. This dowel (when in position) will prevent jib from sliding back into intermediate section.

10. Install part 13 to part 15. The take-up drum should rotate freely. At this point, tie your "cable" (I used 10-lb. fishing line) onto spool after passing it through the boom sections. For a hook, I cast a cylinder of lead and drilled a hole through it for some clothes-hanger wire to pass through. Then I bent the wire to the shape I desired. You can install a screwed eye on the "bumper" of the crane to keep the hook in place when not in use.

11. Now install parts 15 and 12 to part 11. They have to be installed together with the 1"-diameter disc locking the whole assembly in place. The boom should set down in the rest (part 17), with the geared wheel in the crescent-shaped dado.

12. Lastly, install the clothes-hanger wire (look under part 13). You should make the ¾" bend after passing the wire through part 15. This wire will lock into position and act as a stop for the take-up.

Note: The crane shown in Illus. 101 does not agree 100 percent with the working drawings. I made changes in the design after the photo was taken. These changes are reflected in the working drawings.

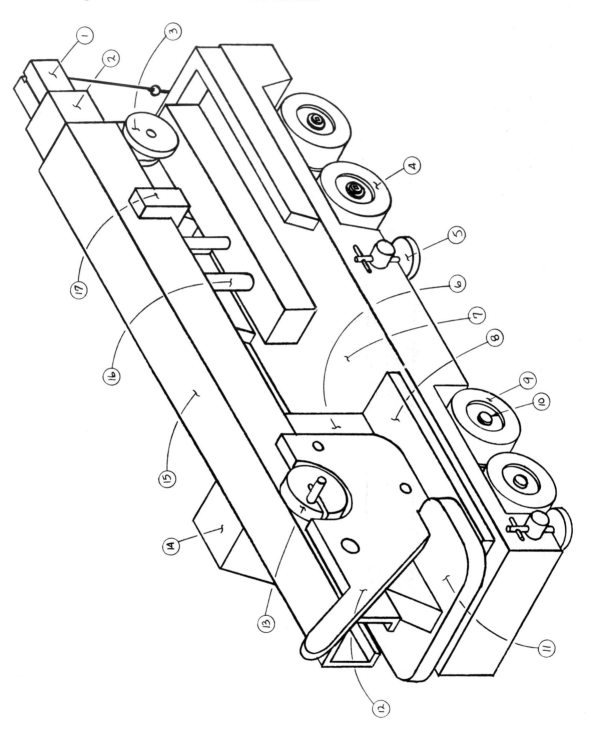

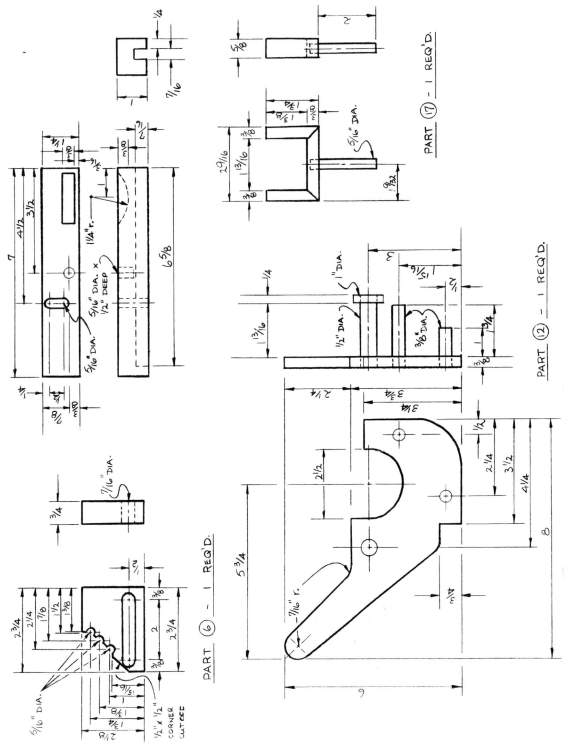

PART ⑰ — 1 REQ'D.

PART ⑫ — 1 REQ'D.

PART ⑥ — 1 REQ'D.

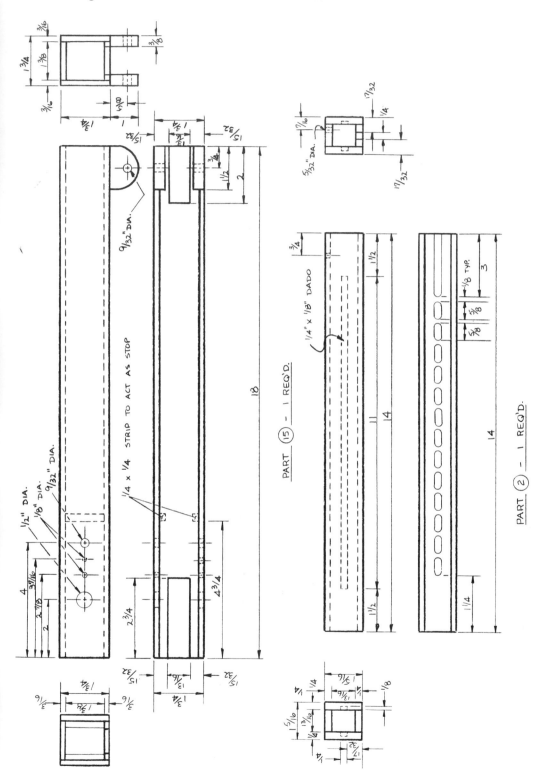

PART ⑮ – 1 REQ'D.

PART ② – 1 REQ'D.

Illus. 104

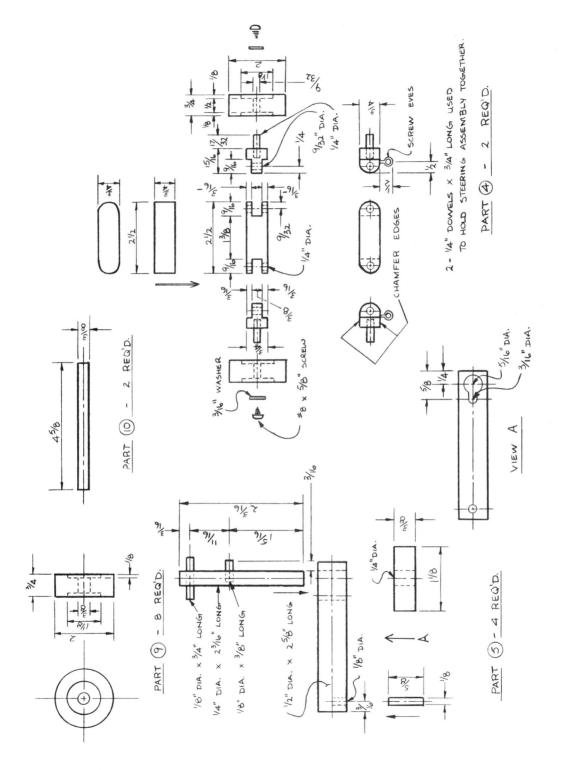

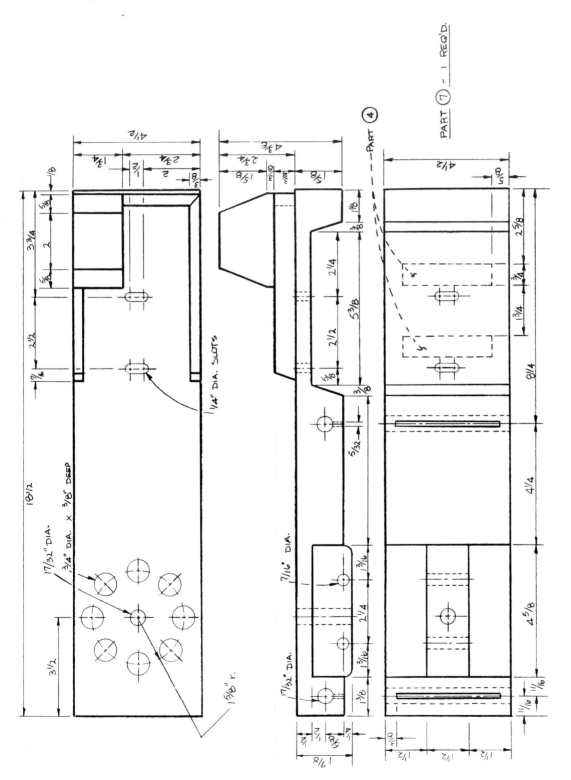

PART 7 – 1 REQ'D.

Illus. 106

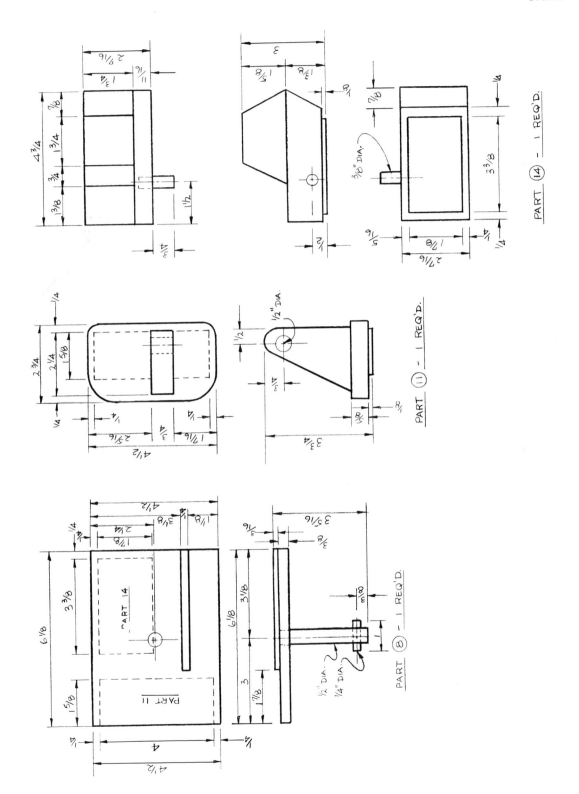

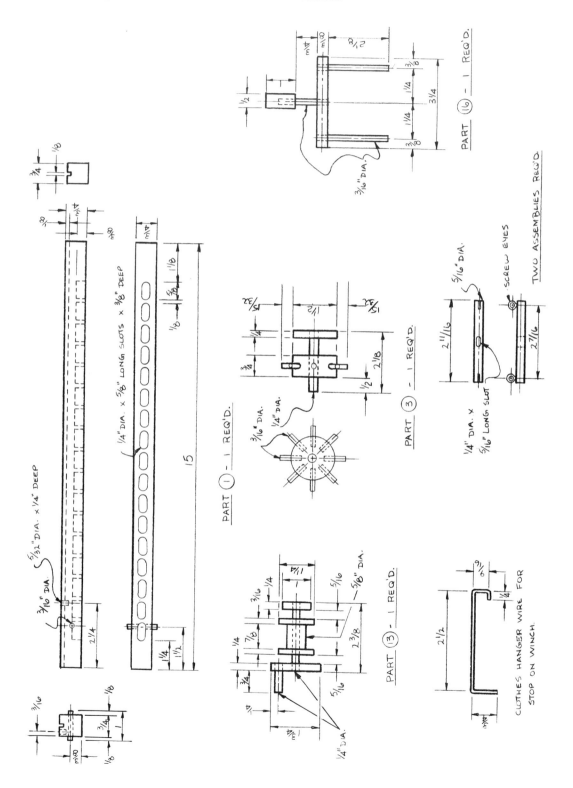

Illus. 109. Loading platform, elevator, unloading ramp, unloading bin, and driving ramp

LOADING PLATFORM

1. Construct the box out of ½" plywood. Add several spacers to the middle section to prevent the top from bowing. Be sure to locate the 1" × ¾" blocks.

2. Glue panelling into place. All joints are mitred.

3. Now make the two cutouts.

4. Construct the connector channel. (You will be installing this later between the elevator and the unloading bin.)

Component Installation:

1. Install elevator. It should fit snugly into place. Do not fasten down because you may need to remove it if marbles should fall into elevator when the lift is up.

2. Place unloading bin into position. Glue or nail into place.

3. Install connector channel. It should fit tightly underneath the bin and up against the elevator. Marbles should be able to drop through bin into channel and run into elevator.

4. Install unloading ramp last. It should fit snugly against unloading bin.

5. Driving ramp is independent of the platform. Top of ramp should come flush with top of platform.

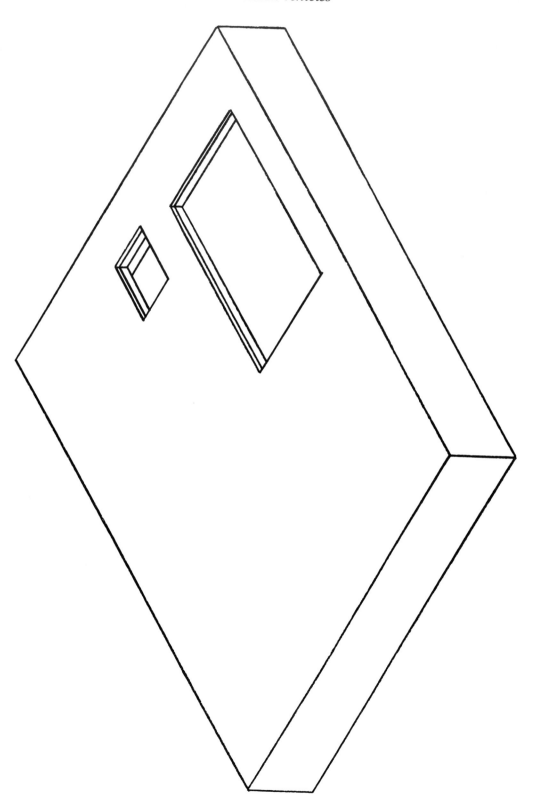

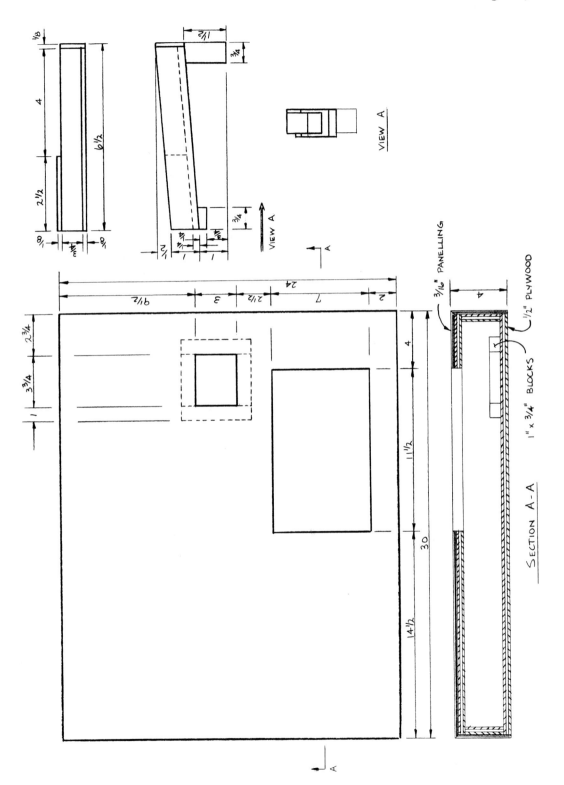

VIEW A

SECTION A-A

3/16" PANELLING

1/2" PLYWOOD

1" x 3/4" BLOCKS

ELEVATOR

1. Construct part 1, making cutouts as required and leaving off top piece.

2. Construct part 3. Drill 1/16"-diameter holes through top of 1/8"-diameter dowels. Run string through these holes diagonally so that it crosses at the center.

3. Construct winch assembly and install into elevator.

4. Place part 3 in position at bottom of elevator. Tie length of string between spool and part 3. (String should be fully unwound on spool when part 3 is in bottom position.)

5. Install top on elevator.

6. Construct part 1. Install to part 2 on angle, as indicated in drawing. Use a 3/8"-diameter dowel to act as brace between bottom of part 1 and side of part 2.

Note: The photograph shows a tin discharge, but later I modified it to all-wood. The working drawings reflect this change.

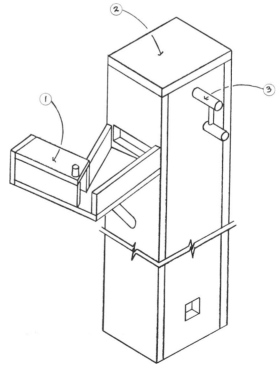

Illus. 112

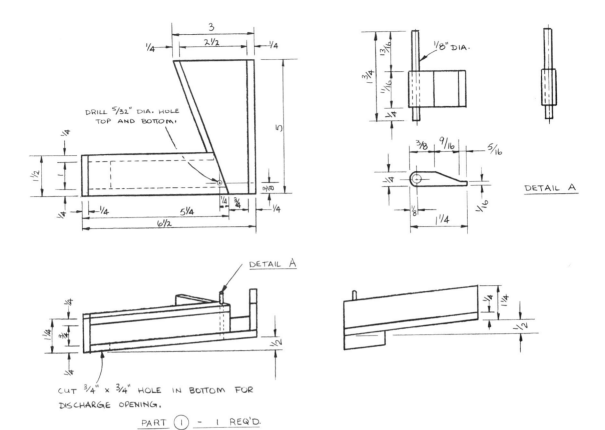

DRILL 5/32" DIA. HOLE
TOP AND BOTTOM.

1/8" DIA.

DETAIL A

DETAIL A

CUT 3/4" × 3/4" HOLE IN BOTTOM FOR
DISCHARGE OPENING.

PART ① - 1 REQ'D.

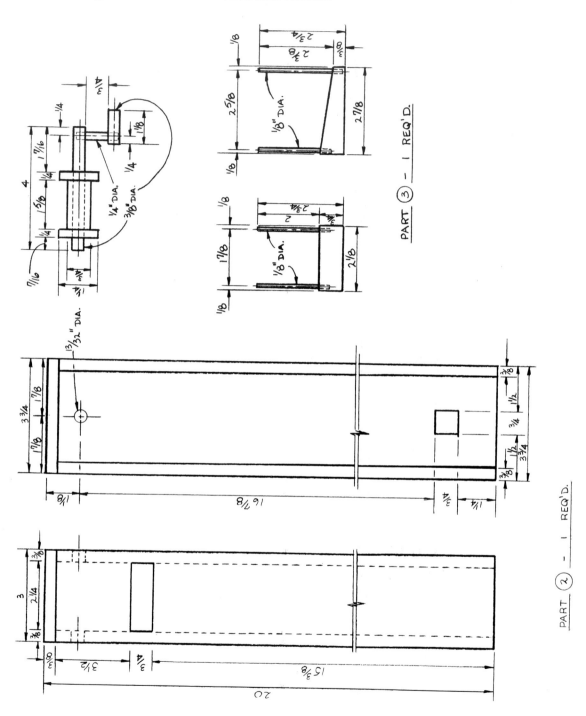

PART ③ — 1 REQ'D.

PART ② — 1 REQ'D.

Illus. 114

UNLOADING RAMP

1. Assemble parts 1, 3, and 4 simultaneously.

2. Glue part 2 into place.

Note: This is the first section of the unloading area. Be sure that the edge of part 1 lines up exactly with the height of part 4 on the unloading bin or else the marbles will hang up on the joint.

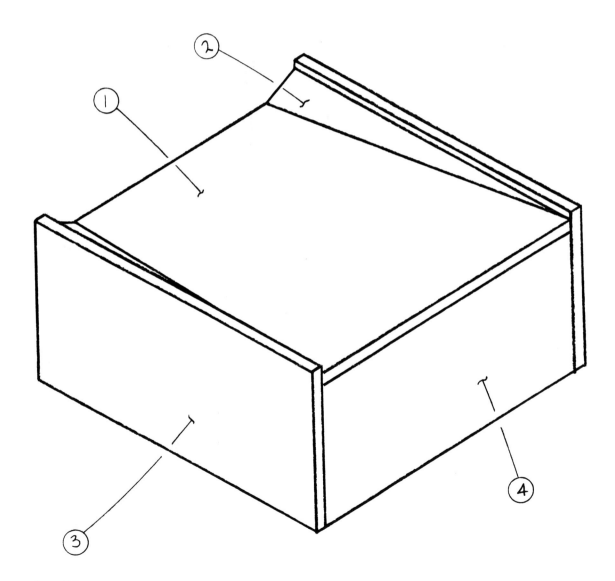

Illus. 115

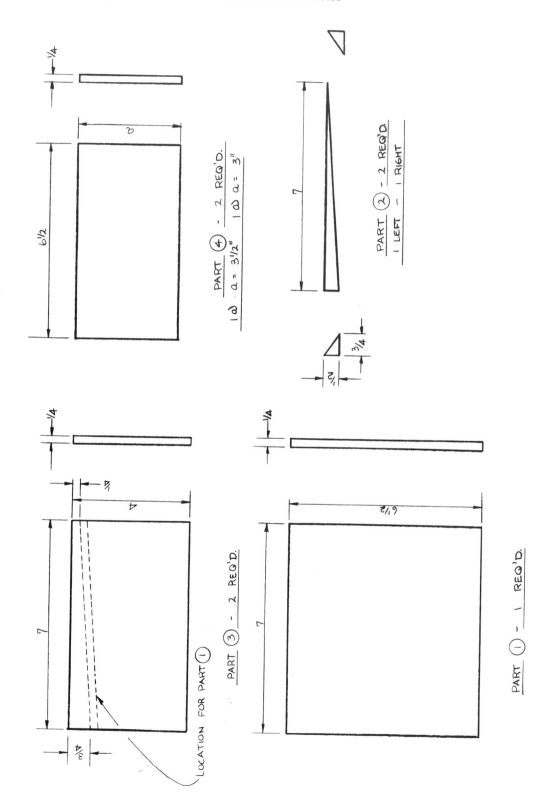

PART ④ - 2 REQ'D.
1 @ . a = 3½"   1 @ a = 3"

PART ② - 2 REQ'D
1 LEFT - 1 RIGHT

PART ③ - 2 REQ'D.
LOCATION FOR PART ①

PART ① - 1 REQ'D.

UNLOADING BIN

1. Assemble parts 1, 2, and 3 simultaneously.

2. Install part 5.

3. Fit and install part 4.

Note: Parts 4 and 5, when installed, form a square discharge hole (¾″ × ¾″), which is ½″ lower than the front edge of part 4.

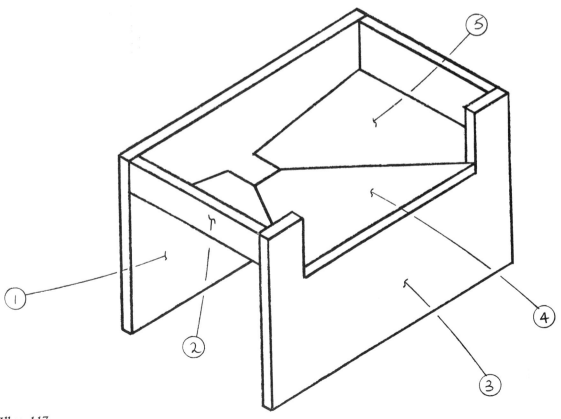

Illus. 117

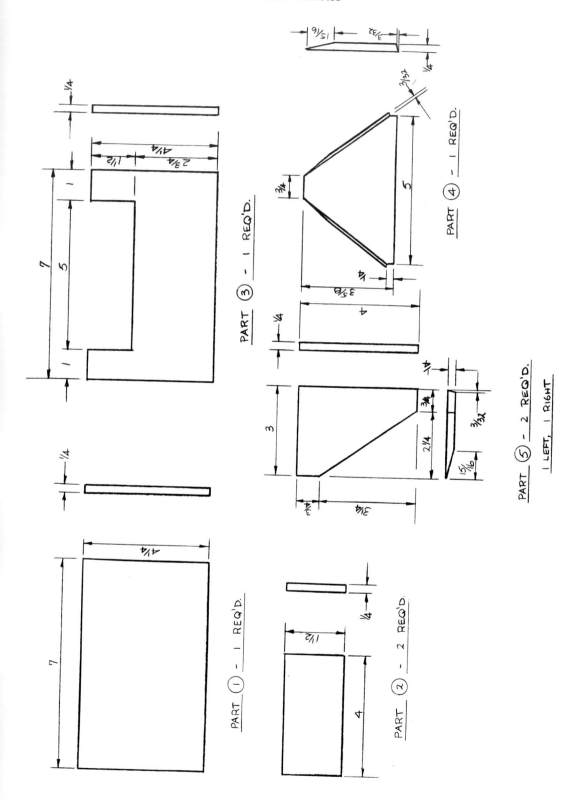

PART ③ – 1 REQ'D.

PART ④ – 1 REQ'D.

PART ⑤ – 2 REQ'D.
1 LEFT, 1 RIGHT

PART ① – 1 REQ'D.

PART ② – 2 REQ'D.

Illus. 118

DRIVING RAMP

1. Cut out the side pieces. You may want to experiment with different patterns to see which will best suit your purposes. The longer the wheel bases of the trucks using the ramp, the easier it will be for them to get hung up on the ramp.

2. Glue the end piece into position. You may also want to install a spacer at the lower end of the ramp until the top piece is in place.

3. Glue or nail the top into place. If you use material thicker than ⅛", adjust the height of the sides and end accordingly. You also might have to "kerf" the top so that it will conform more easily to your pattern. By kerfing I mean making a series of saw cuts to the underside of the top piece approximately halfway through the material. These cuts should run across the width of the top piece for the entire length of the pattern. It should only be necessary to do this if your material is thicker than ⅛". Make sure the grain of the material runs in the direction of the width.

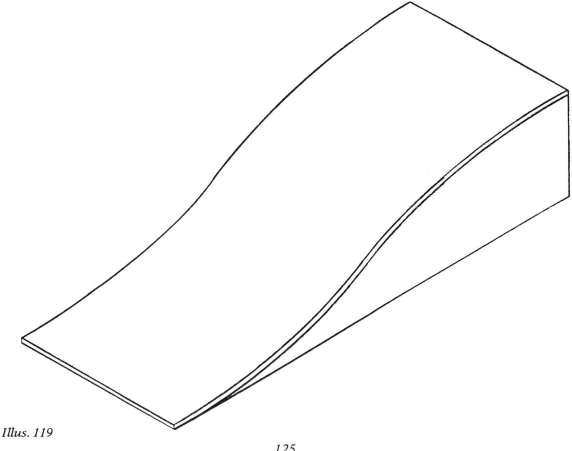

Illus. 119

VIEW A.

2" SQUARES

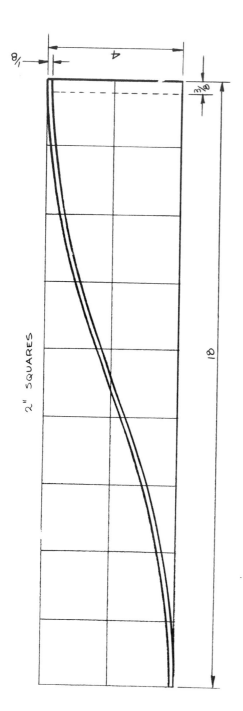

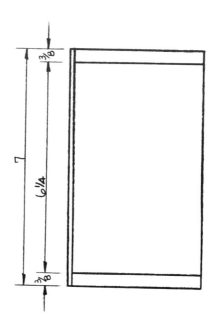

VIEW A

Illus. 120

METRIC EQUIVALENCY CHART

mm—millimetres   **cm**—centimetres

INCHES TO MILLIMETRES AND CENTIMETRES

inches	mm	cm	inches	cm	inches	cm
1/8	3	0.3	9	22.9	30	76.2
1/4	6	0.6	10	25.4	31	78.7
3/8	10	1.0	11	27.9	32	81.3
1/2	13	1.3	12	30.5	33	83.8
5/8	16	1.6	13	33.0	34	86.4
3/4	19	1.9	14	35.6	35	88.9
7/8	22	2.2	15	38.1	36	91.4
1	25	2.5	16	40.6	37	94.0
1 1/4	32	3.2	17	43.2	38	96.5
1 1/2	38	3.8	18	45.7	39	99.1
1 3/4	44	4.4	19	48.3	40	101.6
2	51	5.1	20	50.8	41	104.1
2 1/2	64	6.4	21	53.3	42	106.7
3	76	7.6	22	55.9	43	109.2
3 1/2	89	8.9	23	58.4	44	111.8
4	102	10.2	24	61.0	45	114.3
4 1/2	114	11.4	25	63.5	46	116.8
5	127	12.7	26	66.0	47	119.4
6	152	15.2	27	68.6	48	121.9
7	178	17.8	28	71.1	49	124.5
8	203	20.3	29	73.7	50	127.0

Index